GETTING YOUR SPECIALTY FOOD PRODUCT ONTO STORE SHELVES

The Ultimate Wholesale How-To Guide For Artisan Food Companies

by Jennifer Lewis

ISBN: 0692213287
ISBN 13: 9780692213285

Cover Design By Michelle Draeger

Other Small Food Business Books
Starting A Part-Time Food Business
Food On Wheels
Handmade

Opportunities don't happen, you create them.

~Chris Grosser

TABLE OF CONTENTS

INTRODUCTION

SPECIALTY FOOD, ARTISAN FOOD, HANDCRAFTED food, small-batch food, locally made food—no matter what you call it, there's no question that today's consumers are clamoring for products made by enterprising food entrepreneurs. The growing interest in, and growing sales of, specialty food products has not gone unnoticed by stores. Previously the realm of behemoth brands, today's stores are more willing than ever to add small food brands to their shelves. But just because they're more willing doesn't mean it's easy; it's still an uphill battle for a relatively unknown and underfunded small food company to build a lucrative wholesale business.

This book is aimed at those small food entrepreneurs who want to build or grow the wholesale side of their businesses but don't have millions of dollars to throw at the problem. What this book won't do is give you a "quick-fix, magic formula" (because it doesn't exist) or the "three easy steps" (because it takes more work than that). Neither is this book designed to provide you with surefire recipes, information on the necessary health and business permits needed to start a food business in your specific location, or consumer marketing advice. The sole focus of this book is to provide you with the expertise and information you need so that you can confidently work toward getting your shelf-stable product in front of retail buyers and onto store shelves.

WHY WHOLESALE MATTERS

Before we talk about the specifics, let's take a minute to discuss why a food entrepreneur would want to sell wholesale. If you've chosen to read this book, you probably already know that selling wholesale—which means selling your product to stores (they sell it to their customers)—can be the best way to rapidly increase sales. Instead of selling just one unit to one customer at a time, selling wholesale allows you to sell several units—usually a minimum number set by you—to retailers. Depending on the size of the retailer, this could be six to twelve units at a time or ten thousand units at a time. You can see how just one retailer can have an enormous impact on your bottom line. Assuming your product sells, that retailer will reorder from you again and again as opposed to an individual consumer who may purchase from you occasionally or only once.

Selling wholesale is not just about generating revenue, however. Getting your product onto store shelves can also help build brand recognition. Customers will begin to see and recognize your product. What's more, getting your product onto store shelves (or online or in catalogs) helps to validate your brand and your company for consumers. Think of it this way: before, you may have sold directly to consumers at festivals, markets, and through your online site. To the consumer, this made you a great little company. If that consumer also happens to see your product at his or her favorite store or in a respected catalog, he or she might suddenly view your brand as much more valuable. This type of exposure makes you and your company seem more trustworthy to the consumer, as the consumer essentially believes that you've already been vetted by retailers. What retailer would risk its reputation on a product it didn't believe in? This exposure also encourages consumers who might not try your product otherwise to be willing to try it. If all goes well, that consumer will buy your product again and again, eventually becoming an advocate for your company and spreading the word about your product to friends and family.

Increased sales, increased distribution, and increased brand recognition: does this sound like what you're looking for? Then let's start by taking a look at the wholesale food landscape and making sure we understand who all the players are.

CHAPTER 1

UNDERSTANDING THE WHOLESALE LANDSCAPE

MOST SPECIALTY FOOD BUSINESSES BEGIN by selling directly to the consumer. This might include having booths at farmers' markets or selling online through the business's own website or through a partner site like Etsy.com or Shopify.com.

Since selling wholesale entails selling to stores who then sell to the customer, that end consumer is no longer your sole concern when you're trying to build your wholesale business (though, obviously, you always want to keep that end customer in mind!). To get your products onto store shelves in the first place, you need to understand the roles of three key players in the wholesale food industry: the buyers, the brokers, and the distributors. All of these people or business entities perform different functions in the industry, some or all of which you may encounter at some time. As such, it makes sense to understand the role each plays as you grow your wholesale business.

CUSTOMERS

DIRECT RETAIL

Depending on what type of business you have, many entrepreneurs start by selling direct to customers. This might be a sale you make at a farmers' market or festival, an online order you receive, or someone purchasing from your own retail storefront. In all of those cases you are selling directly to the end consumer and charging them your retail price point.

BUYERS

Anytime you sell into a store, you will, at some level or another, be working with the store's buyer. Sometimes also known as category managers, buyers are the people who decide which products the store brings onto its shelves and which it takes off. No matter whether you want to get your products into brick-and-mortar stores, online stores, or mail-order catalogs, buyers make the ultimate decision on who makes the cut and who doesn't.

Whole Foods Market is notoriously decentralized when it comes to buying. Though they have national, regional, and even specific store buyers, the organization has also empowered its employees so that, should an employee who isn't a buyer find what he or she thinks is an interesting product that would appeal to customers, he or she is encouraged to bring the product before the store buyers. In cases like this, the product is usually brought in at the store level and then, if it performs well, it may be brought into other stores in the region and potentially even nationally. From the standpoint of large supermarkets, though, Whole Foods Market is the exception to the rule. Most supermarkets don't encourage their baggers to bring them new product ideas.

That's not to say that all buyer positions are alike. Depending on the size of the store, the buyer may be juggling several distinct responsibilities. This is often the case with independently owned retail stores where the buyer is the store owner and is also responsible for stocking shelves, managing employees, doing all the bookkeeping, and overseeing the marketing. In other stores, the buyer is its own separate position charged with and evaluated on determining which products and brands to bring into the store. In some cases, these buyers are responsible for all of the purchasing for an entire store; in others, especially in larger supermarkets, there may be several buyers or category managers, each of whom is responsible for different sections of the store. To take it one step further, some large stores and national chains have centralized buyers who make all the buying decisions for the entire company regardless of where the stores are located. Yet other large stores leave the buying decisions to regional buyers or may even have specific, store-level buyers.

Why is this important? Whether you work directly with the buyer through what's known as direct store delivery or DSD or you work through a food broker or distributor (we will talk more about the specific roles of food brokers and distributors later in this chapter), at the end of the day, it is the buyers who control your fate and who decide whether or not your products go onto their shelves. Therefore, you need to understand what buyers are looking for and what is important to them. Obviously, food products being delicious and safe for consumption is these buyers' primary concern, but that's not all they're looking at when they evaluate your products.

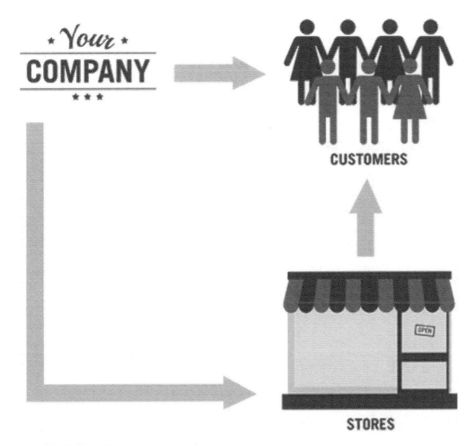

DIRECT STORE DELIVERY

Getting your product onto others' store shelves means that you are now selling wholesale. In the case of direct store delivery (DSD) you work with the buyer from that store and ship or drop off their orders to them. Because they will need to mark the product up in order to make money, they will want to know what your wholesale price is.

Direct store delivery (DSD) is a method of selling wholesale in which you work directly with the store's buyer, not through an intermediary like a food broker or distributor. It works just as it sounds: you deliver the products directly to the store, perhaps dropping them off in person or shipping them to the store.

Criteria Buyers Use to Make Purchasing Decisions

HOW WILL THIS FIT ON MY SHELF?

For a small, independent retailer, the concern may be how your product fits with the overall look and feel of the store. For example, buyers for high-end stores want packaging with a high-end look and feel. While buyers for other types of establishments are less concerned with the overall connection of your packaging to their brands, they still want your product to look good on their shelves. To them, this means it must fit on a normal-size supermarket shelf. They are concerned with how much space one product facing takes up. You can never forget that retailers have a specific amount of "real estate"—shelf space—and they want to maximize the profit from that space. If your packaging is twice the size of a competitor's, taking up twice the shelf space, can it generate twice the profit for the supermarket to make up for its lost real estate?

HOW FAST WILL THIS SELL?

Usually referred to as "turns" in the retail industry, buyers check how quickly their inventory of a specific product sells through or how often it "turns" in one year. The faster a product turns, the higher the demand, and not surprisingly, the more likely buyers want to keep it in stock and on the shelf. Obviously, you should aim to create products that have high turns. This not only helps keep your product in stores, but it also means you'll sell greater quantities to keep up with their demand.

HOW MUCH PROFIT WILL WE MAKE PER SALE?

Retail buyers are concerned with the gross margin return on investment. Said another way, they calculate how much they make selling something for $Y if they buy it for $X before they take into account their other overhead costs. For example, your product costs $5 per unit and they sell it for $9. Their gross profit is $4 and they have a 45 percent gross margin. A good buyer measures this margin against similar competing products to maximize potential earnings. (More about how to calculate margins and pricing is in chapter 3).

There are certainly other metrics that buyers and stores use to determine what products should be on their shelves. Some stores, you may find, have very strict formulas, such as a minimum 45 percent gross margin for every item in inventory. You may find some buyers who are judged on one or two metrics and thus judge your product accordingly, whereas other buyers simply bring on a product because they like it or because they think it fills a hole in their store's product offerings, even if it's not highly lucrative.

Since what buyers are looking for can vary widely based on store type, the "Selling To" chapters starting with chapter 11 offer more in-depth discussion of the subject.

FOOD BROKERS

For those food artisans who want to open up wholesale accounts, the biggest deterrent may be finding the time to go out and meet with appropriate store buyers. You must identify which stores you want to be in, contact the right people within the organization, find time to meet with them, sell them on your product's benefits, and share samples with them. Then, if things go well, perhaps you'll open one new wholesale account. It's easy to see how time-consuming this process can be. For many small food businesses, pursuing new wholesale accounts can be hard given all the other day-to-day aspects of running the business. So, if you want to sell wholesale to a number of businesses, you may need to get more bodies to help you. This is where food brokers may come in handy.

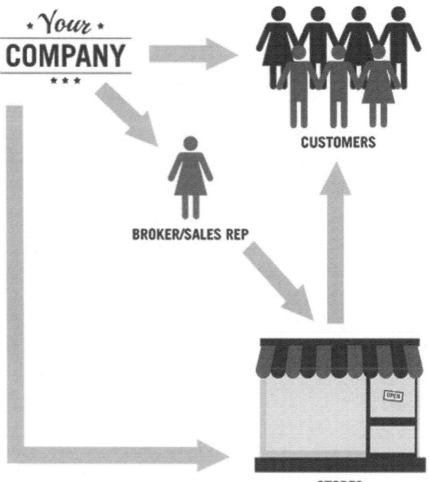

BROKERS/SALES REPS

As a small business you likely don't have a dedicated sales team that can go out and call on all the retailers you hope to get your product into which is where brokers/sales representatives can come into play. These individuals are independent of your company and they represent a number of products and brands usually within a defined geographic territory; leveraging existing relationships they have with retailers to get orders. Typically, brokers/sales reps don't carry any product inventory themselves and you are responsible for shipping the orders to the retailers. Brokers/sales reps are paid a commission on the sales of your products they make to stores.

Food brokers, sometimes also called food reps, essentially act as independent salespeople for a number of different products and brands that they market to various store buyers and, in some cases, to distributors. Typically, a food broker works in a particular geographic territory in which he or she has established relationships with buyers. Such relationships may be with large regional or national supermarket chains, or the broker may specialize in one or more niche markets, like high-end retail boutiques, health food stores, specialty-food stores, gift shops, and so on.

Food brokers operate by approaching stores with product brochures and samples from the companies they represent. When a buyer is interested in a product, the food broker shares the wholesale price set by the food manufacturer. Food brokers, who are independent salespeople, make agreed-upon commissions from food manufacturers as a percentage of an order's sales revenue. This means that the food broker sends the store's order to you; you fill and ship it, and you bill the store for the order. The food broker then later bills you for the commission based on the order amount.

Brokers, as you can see, are incentivized to sell your product because they get paid based on how many of your products they sell. This is just one reason, as you'll see in the next chapter, why setting your price points correctly is so important. It's worth noting, however, that although the way in which food brokers are paid encourages them to get as many orders as possible, they are also incentivized to spend the most time and attention showcasing the top-selling brands in their portfolios since those products bring the broker more income. This means that a broker may be unwilling to take on your products, or may jettison them or may pay less attention to them if they are slower to sell. While this can be unnerving for some entrepreneurs, the upside is that most brokers want to present buyers with new and unique products and will hopefully give your brand a fair shot.

We'll talk about pricing and commission structures for food brokers in the next chapter and more details about how to find and work with them (including what to look for and how to find the right broker for your business) in the chapter titled "Working with Food Brokers."

DISTRIBUTORS

Like food brokers, distributors try to get your products onto more store shelves, but unlike them, distributors take on some of the inventory risk. Distributors buy products directly from you and hold them in their warehouses. Their sales teams show your products to the companies they work with, along with the other products the distributors sell. When a store places an order, the distributor oversees the logistics of transporting the products from the warehouse to the store.

Distributors expect to be compensated for the inventory risk they take, for coordinating logistics, and the use of their sales team to help sell your specialty food products. But, like food brokers, they also want to offer their customers the best possible wholesale prices. They do this by asking you for what's called a "distributor price." As with all pricing, this isn't just a number you can pull out of thin air. Distributors want to offer your product to their retail customers at your normal wholesale price; therefore, the distributor price is *below* your wholesale price. The distributor makes money by marking your products up to the wholesale price and pocketing the difference.

The next chapter covers price points and how to arrive at them in more detail, while the "Working with Distributors" chapter provides more specifics about the role of distributors in the food industry and what you need to know about finding and working with them.

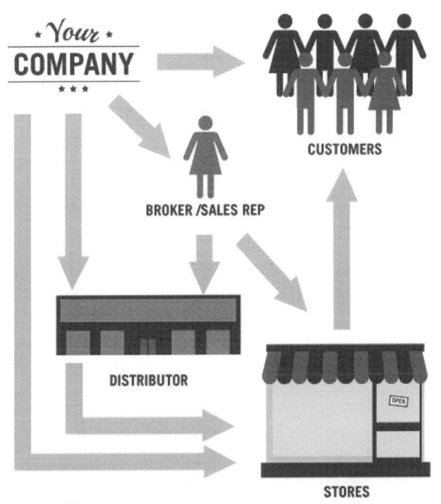

DISTRIBUTORS

As you grow, especially if you hope to work with supermarkets or chain stores, you will likely need to add distributors to your sales mix. Like brokers, who do sometimes help you get accounts with distributors, distributors have a selection of products in their portfolio and they help get those products onto store shelves. Unlike brokers though, distributors will buy inventory from you and hold it in their warehouse. They are also responsible for the transportation of that product from their warehouse to the stores when an order is placed. For that inventory risk and the value of their sales relationships and operational logistics, distributors are most often compensated by being offered a distributor price that is lower than the wholesale price offered to buyers and brokers/sales reps.

SPEAKING THE LANGUAGE OF BUYERS

Going forward, I will refer to retail buyers, brokers, and distributors collectively as "buyers." If this is your first foray into wholesale selling, then some of the words buyers toss around can seem like another language. The lingo presented below is by no means a complete list of wholesale terms. This is simply a compilation of the words that you, as a small business owner, are most likely to hear. You'll want to ensure that you understand these basic terms at a minimum, but if a buyer uses a phrase you're not familiar with, make sure you find out what they're specifically asking for before agreeing to any contracts.

CASE PACK: Typically, in wholesale, units of product are sold by the case pack. This refers to how many products fit into a standard shipping box. For example, you may determine that your case pack contains twelve units. Buyers then calculate how many cases they need to get the total units they want.

CERTIFICATE OF LIABILITY: Most buyers, especially in larger stores, require you to have liability insurance and that you add their store to a policy rider before they carry your product. You may have to fill out a certificate of liability (sometimes simply referred to as a COL) to document your addition of the retailer as an additional insured to your liability insurance policy.

DROP-SHIP: Often used by online stores and catalog companies, drop-shipping means a retailer offers certain products without actually carrying them in inventory. The retailer forwards each consumer order to the food company, who then ships the product directly to the consumer. The food company charges the retailer its wholesale price, and the retailer makes money on the difference charged to the consumer. More information about drop-shipping is in the Selling To Catalogues chapter.

FREIGHT ON BOARD (FOB): FOB identifies who is responsible for shipping costs—either you or the buyer. Equally as important, this also identifies where liability falls with regard to goods transfer. For example, if the buyer is responsible for the shipping, then as soon as the product leaves the entrepreneur's hands, the product liability and risk fall to the buyer. Typically, the phrase "FOB origin" indicates that the buyer is responsible for shipping costs and liability, whereas "FOB destination" means that the food business covers shipping costs and remains responsible for the product until it arrives at the buyer's store.

TERMS: "Terms" refers to the order payment specifics the seller and buyer agree on. They can specify what forms of payment are accepted, when you expect to be paid, who covers the cost of shipping, order lead time, or any other specifics related to the sale. Ideally, your terms should be included on your wholesale order form, although some buyers may want to negotiate the terms.

NET 15/30/60: Technically, any talk of net payment is included as part of the terms, but buyers often use phrases like "Net 15," "Net 30," or "Net 60." They refer to the number of days after an order is received by the buyer before the buyer is required to pay you. For example, "Net 30" means that the buyer must submit payment no later than thirty days after the order was received. You may also see or hear phrases like "2/10 Net 30," which means that the buyer receives a 2 percent discount if the bill is paid within the first ten days, but that full payment is required within thirty days in any case. Some businesses use this approach to motivate their buyers to pay sooner rather than later.

MANUFACTURER'S SUGGESTED RETAIL PRICE (MSRP): The MSRP is the retail price at which you recommend that your products be sold. While buyers aren't required to charge the MSRP, they want to know what price you recommend. You may also see the term SRP, which is exactly the same thing but without the word "manufacturer's" in it.

MINIMUM ORDER: A minimum order is the lowest dollar amount, case amount, or unit amount that a buyer can purchase. It prohibits buyers from placing an order so small that it's not worth your time to fill. You set your own minimum amounts for each product depending on what works best for you.

POINT-OF-PURCHASE (POP): You may have heard this term in regard to a store's checkout process, but technically, that is point-of-sale (POS). Though many use the terms interchangeably, there is a difference. If a buyer asks you whether there is any POP available, he or she is asking about any graphics, display units, or other visuals that retail stores can exhibit. POP can take the form of posters, placards, or other pieces of marketing material that help draw the attention of the consumer and inform them about the product in the hope of increased purchasing.

PRIVATE LABEL: It is not uncommon for buyers to ask small food businesses if they are willing to produce private-label products for them. Sometimes called "store brands," these products are identical or similar to a food manufacturer's existing product. However, the private-label product is marketed under the retailer's brand, and the retailer takes all responsibility for its marketing, shelf placement, and promotion.

CHAPTER 2

DEVELOPING A STRATEGIC AND PROFITABLE PRICING STRUCTURE

AS YOU NOW KNOW, THERE are many different ways you can get your products onto store shelves. You can work directly with store buyers, you can partner with food brokers, you can sign up with distributors—and many food entrepreneurs work with more than one of these at a time. Of course, you'll need to quote your buyers a wholesale price point that works for them—and for you.

In many cases, the specialty food entrepreneurs I talk with are already selling their products to consumers via farmers' markets, festivals, pop-up stores, online storefronts, or even in small brick-and-mortar spaces of their own. Even when food businesses have already established a retail price point, I recommend they work through the following pricing exercises. Often, food entrepreneurs discover that they're not charging a high enough retail price to accommodate wholesale and distributor pricing: there's not enough built-in profit margin. If you're serious about selling wholesale as a significant revenue stream, you need to ensure that your pricing structure has enough room in it so that all players—the stores themselves, the food brokers, the distributors, and you—are making a healthy gross profit.

The Difference between Net and Gross Profit

As soon as any discussion of accounting begins, phrases like net and gross are tossed about so often that you might think they're interchangeable. The difference between them is huge, though, and it's critical that you understand it.

Gross profit is a calculation that only counts the difference between the cost of making the product and what you charge for it. If it costs you $1 to make and you sell it for $6, $5 is your gross profit.

Net profit goes a step further. It includes the cost of making a product but adds all the other costs of running your business. These are things like overhead costs (such as your electric bill and phone bill), your administrative costs, and your sales and marketing costs. Using the above example, you may have a gross profit of $5, but if all your other costs add up to $3, then your net profit is $2.

The terms "net" and "gross" aren't limited to analysis of profit. It's common for food producers and buyers to calculate their gross and net margins as well.

THE FOOD INDUSTRY IS A MARGINS GAME

Unless you come from a sales or accounting background, you might be confused about the meanings of "markup" and "margin." Like many other terms, we often hear them used interchangeably, but they mean very different things. In the food industry, everyone you interact with—buyers, brokers, and distributors—are concerned with and will ask about your margins, so it makes sense to spend a minute to understand the difference between them and how each is calculated.

You may hear, "That store really marks up its products." What does that actually mean? Technically, a markup is a percentage added to the cost of a product to derive the selling price. For example, a cheese retailer that wants to have a minimum 50 percent markup on every product in the store would determine pricing this way for a block of cheese that costs him $5 to purchase:

$$\$5 \times 50\% = \$2.50$$
$$\$5 + \$2.50 = \$7.50$$

Therefore, the retailer charges $7.50 per unit of cheese to make $2.50 from each sale.

"Margin" is the profit from a sale after costs have been taken into account, expressed as a percentage. "Gross margin" considers only costs directly related to product creation (such as ingredients, packaging, and labor), whereas "net margin" takes into account all business expenses including overhead and administrative.

In the food industry, pricing focuses on gross margin. The costs that are directly related to the production of the product are also known as your "cost of goods sold." You subtract them from your price and then divide that difference by the price:

$$\frac{(\text{Price} - \text{Cost})}{\text{Price}}$$

So, the retailer that buys cheese for $5 and sells it for $7.50 has a gross margin of 33 percent:

$$\frac{(\$7.50 - \$5.00)}{\$7.50} = 33\%$$

As you can see, even though these margins are based on the same numbers, the calculations are different. Our cheese retailer has a *markup* of 50 percent and a *gross margin* of 33 percent. You need to understand the difference, because in the food world, we're playing a margins game.

Margins are what all experienced food manufacturers, distributors, brokers, and retailers are focused on and will ask you about. You need to create a price structure that allows all players in the industry to have healthy margins—including yourself! Ensuring that you have healthy gross margins, as we'll discuss in more detail, gives you enough cash to cover your direct production costs *and* your daily business costs.

CALCULATING YOUR COST OF GOODS SOLD

Before you can start figuring out your price points, you must have a firm grasp on what it costs to produce your products. For food businesses, the "cost of goods sold" (COGS) includes your ingredient costs, packaging costs, and labor costs that are directly related to the production of your product. Having only a rough idea of your COGS is a very dangerous financial game. It's common for entrepreneurs who guesstimate costs to underestimate them. That puts them at risk for underpricing their products, which at the very least means they are pocketing less profit for each unit sold. That's money that could be used in other parts of the business such as advertising, overhead, or the business owner's salary!

> You may prefer to work through product costing on an Excel worksheet. You can download one at smallfoodbiz.com that can even recommend pricing based on your preferred margins.

Since each of the products you produce has a different set of costs, you need to have a to-the-penny understanding of each product's COGS. To calculate them, you must walk step by step through your recipes, determining your unit costs for each ingredient as well as your packaging and labor costs. The following example walks through the steps of how a fictional company, Aunt B's Jams, calculates the costs for one of its products. You'll also find a worksheet that you can use to calculate your own products' COGS.

Product Costing
(Aunt B's Jams)

Product Name:

Strawberry Vanilla Jam

Basic Materials Cost

Strawberries = $3.29 per quart

Sugar = $.67 per pound

Vanilla Beans = $38/100 beans = $.38 per bean

Lemons = $1.09 per lemon

Liquid Pectin = $2.99/12 oz = $.25 per oz

Pint Jars = $5.99/12 jars = $.49 per jar

Labels = $11.75/100 labels = $.11 per label

Product Raw Materials Cost

2 quarts × $3.29 = $6.58

1 × $.67 = $.67

2 vanilla beans × $.38 = $.76

2 lemons × $1.09 = $2.18

6 ounces × $.25 = $1.50

4 jars × $.49 = $1.96

4 labels × $.11 = $.44

Total Associated Raw Materials Cost = $14.09

Total Labor Cost = $24.00

(It takes Aunt B's 2 hours to make this jam at $12.00/hr)

Total Product Cost = $38.09

In this case, this Total Product Cost refers to the total cost to make 4 jars so the cost per jar cost is $9.52.

Product Costing

Product Name:

_____

Basic Raw Materials Cost	Product Raw Materials Cost
_____	_____
_____	_____
_____	_____
_____	_____
_____	_____
_____	_____
_____	_____
_____	_____

Total Associated Raw Materials Cost _____

Total Labor Cost _____

Total Product Cost _____

Per piece cost if more than one unit is produced at a time _____

CALCULATING YOUR WHOLESALE PRICE

Once you know how much it costs you to make your products, you can use that information to calculate your wholesale price. That's right, I said wholesale price—not your retail price. Your retail price point, the price that consumers pay, should be built on your wholesale price, not the other way around. This is where many specialty food entrepreneurs get into trouble. When you try to calculate your wholesale price from your retail price, you run an enormous risk of leaving yourself with little to no margin. When the wholesale price is calculated first and then the retail price from that, you ensure that your margin is on track to help cover the other important aspects of your business, like your overhead and administrative expenses.

Making sure you have enough margin for these items is important, especially as you start to work with distributors or when you start offering promotions or discounts off of your price points. Both of these will cut into your profits. You want to make sure that your business has the room to grow as needed but also has the cash available to finance that growth!

Although every product category differs somewhat, you should ideally have a minimum margin of 50 percent as you calculate your wholesale price. This helps ensure that the wholesale price you arrive at not only includes the costs that you've calculated as part of your COGS but also the other business expenses your company faces every day.

Let's look at an example of how wholesale prices are calculated using margins. A food entrepreneur's Cost of Goods Sold is $2.50 per unit of product; the ideal margin, in this case, is 55 percent. With these numbers, the wholesale price is calculated this way:

$$\text{cost} / (1 - \text{ideal margin})$$
$$\$2.50 / (1 - .55) = \$5.56$$

In this example, the food entrepreneur is going to make $3.06 on every unit of product that she or he sells wholesale:

$$\$5.56 - \$2.50 = \$3.06$$

It's worth noting that in this example, the wholesale price does not include things like the cost to ship or drop off the product to the retailer. Though omission of these expenses in setting wholesale price is not uncommon, here the entrepreneur should clearly convey that shipping or freight expenses must be added to arrive at the retailer's final price.

CALCULATING YOUR MANUFACTURER'S SUGGESTED RETAIL PRICE

Now that you've calculated wholesale prices for each product, you can use them to help you determine what the right manufacturers' suggested retail price (MSRP) should be. Keep in mind that although buyers will ask what your MSRPs are, buyers are free to price your products above or below that amount once the product is in their control. As I've noted, you should never undermine your retailers by pricing your own retail sales well below your MSRP; this is considered bad form and can quickly lose you wholesale accounts.

> **Determining Your Ideal Retail Margin**
>
> Unless you're selling a highly specialized product or one that requires special storage (such as refrigeration or freezer space which an added expense for the retailer), it is usually safe to assume a 50 percent retail margin when calculating your retail price point.

To calculate your MSRP, you use the same margin calculation formula as in determining your wholesale prices, but instead of using your COGS as your base cost, you'll use your wholesale price. We calculated that the wholesale price for our food entrepreneur's product was $5.56. Aiming for an ideal retailer margin of 50%, we arrive at the MSRP this way:

$$\text{cost} / (1 - \text{ideal margin})$$
$$\$5.56 / (1 - .50) = \$11.12$$

I'll give you a minute to consider how a product that costs you $2.50 to make can end up costing the customer $11.12 to purchase. Oftentimes, entrepreneurs realize that they won't be making as much money selling wholesale as they would selling directly to customers based on the suggested retail price they've calculated. Therefore, many determine that selling wholesale isn't the right path for them. Keep in mind, though, that in addition to the many benefits of selling wholesale, you are not required to focus your energy exclusively either on wholesale or retail. You can do a combination, which enables you to enjoy the best of both worlds—the quantities and repeat sales of wholesale accounts and the higher profit of selling retail.

CALCULATING YOUR BROKER PRICE

As I've noted, food brokers, as outside sales representatives for your company, are traditionally paid by commission. This means that you must educate the broker on your products' wholesale prices. Brokers don't actually add any costs to your price when shopping your product to buyers or category managers; the broker bills you for your agreed-upon percentage of each sale.

> In the past few years, more brokers have been asking for monthly retainers in addition to commission. Some brokers are worth it, especially if they offer you services above and beyond simply opening and maintaining account relationships or if they have relationships with key buyers. That being said, you should be wary of agreeing to a monthly retainer unless you are sure the broker will provide you with a high level of sales. At the very worst, if this is a broker you simply have to have, ask him or her to work on a commission-only basis for a few months to prove to you the level of sales generation you want, after which you can move to a retainer-and-commission structure.

As in any negotiated contract, commission rates vary widely, so be prepared to put on your best negotiating hat as you work out agreements. There is an industry average, though: food broker commissions average 10 to 15 percent of sales when he or she works directly with buyers and 5 to 10 percent when selling to distributors. The number also varies with type of product as well as the broker's industry experience and contacts.

Clearly, our example product that cost $2.50 to make and the entrepreneur sold for a wholesale price of $5.56 cannot net $3.06 under the broker model. Assuming a broker commission of 12 percent, the calculation of gross profit now comes out this way:

$$\$5.56 \times .12 = \$.67 \text{ (Broker Commission)}$$
$$\$3.06 - \$.67 = \$2.39 \text{ (Producer Profit)}$$

Remember, the $.67 broker commission in this example is paid on every unit the broker sells. You can see now why healthy wholesale margins make a big difference. It's easy for margins to get squeezed!

More information about establishing and maintaining broker relationships can be found in the Working with Food Brokers chapter.

CALCULATING DISTRIBUTOR PRICING

We've already noted that distributors take inventory risk by holding product in warehouses and include services such as coordinating transportation logistics and sales teams. The "distributor price" they pay for your items enables them to offer your wholesale price to store buyers while covering their own costs plus providing them with a profit. As discussed, this means that the distributor price is below your wholesale price.

Consider that concept again: the distributor price is *below* your wholesale price. You can see why setting a retail price haphazardly in the beginning can have a negative, cascading effect throughout your pricing channels. Poorly set pricing can prohibit you from working with distributors.

So, how much lower than the wholesale price should the distributor price be? As with most things in the food industry, there are no hard-and-fast numbers; distributors vary in their margins, and your product category is also a factor. That being said, a good ballpark figure to start with is 25 to 30 percent.

Calculate your distributor price with the same formula as before, this time using the distributor margin. Starting with a wholesale price of $5.56 and a distributor margin of 30 percent, we calculate:

$$\text{Wholesale Price} *$$
$$(1 - \text{ideal distributor margin})$$
$$\$5.56 * (1 - .30) = \$3.89$$

So, the entrepreneur charges a distributor $3.89 per unit versus a wholesale price of $5.56. A distributor makes money based on the difference between the price you charge (the distributor price) and the wholesale price:

$$\$5.56 - \$3.89 = \$1.67 \text{ (Distributor Profit)}$$

Of course, the money the entrepreneur makes here is the distributor price less the COGS:

$$\$3.89 - \$2.50 = \$1.39 \text{ (Producer Profit)}$$

Even though this profit is significantly lower than what the food entrepreneur could make selling directly to a store (and certainly much lower than by selling retail to customers), the right distributor can help you get into stores that you might not otherwise be able to work with.

A more detailed description of working with distributors starts in chapter 10.

Common Pricing Questions

WHAT IF MY CALCULATED RETAIL PRICE POINT IS SO HIGH THAT A CUSTOMER WOULD NEVER PAY IT?

If you feel that your retail price point is too high after taking into account your distributor and wholesale pricing, you should look for ways to lower your COGS. You may also consider lowering your margins, but remember that doing so is giving up money you could be using to grow your business or pay yourself.

If it's not possible to lower your product costs or margin, you should investigate whether your business model and your plan to sell wholesale are the best for your product. You may be better suited for selling directly to customers at a price point that works for that channel. Without the additional middlemen of brokers, buyers, and distributors to account for, you have more flexibility in pricing your product and increased profitability.

WHAT IF MY CALCULATED PRICE POINTS SEEM TOO LOW? CUSTOMERS ARE WILLING TO PAY MORE THAN THAT FOR PRODUCTS LIKE MINE!

Calculate your prices using margins, but always review how your competitors price their products. If you find that their products are priced higher, you have an advantage: you have the option to increase your own prices, thus increasing your margin and your profit for each unit sold, or to sell at a lower price than your competitors do. However, do keep in mind that sometimes, a lower price point can mean "lower quality" in consumers' minds.

WHAT IF I'M ALREADY SELLING AT A CERTAIN RETAIL PRICE POINT?

It's not unusual for a food entrepreneur to start by selling direct to customers and then want to move to selling wholesale, only to find that their retail prices are not high enough to cover the costs of selling wholesale. If this is you, you'll need to weigh the costs and benefits of adjusting your retail price point and potentially upsetting regular customers against changing your recipe to use cheaper ingredients while trying to maintain quality. Ultimately, you may determine that selling wholesale is not a viable strategy for you for that product. That doesn't keep you from creating a new product, either now or down the road, that you can price appropriately and bring into retail stores.

CHAPTER 3

KNOWING YOUR MARKET

IT'S HARD, IF NOT IMPOSSIBLE, to get and keep your products on retail store shelves in this highly competitive industry unless you take the time to understand the market landscape and how you fit into it compared to your competitors.

UNDERSTANDING THE INDUSTRY

The first step toward knowing your market is understanding the industry as a whole and how it is changing. The Specialty Food Trade Association (www.specialtyfood.com) conducts annual studies in collaboration with Mintel Research that can provide you with background information on how the specialty food industry as a whole is faring and how sales of specialty food products have risen or fallen in the last year. There are also numerous online sites and news outlets, including the Small Food Business site (www.smallfoodbiz.com), that can help you understand trends and changes in the specialty food industry.

It's also worthwhile to research how your subcategory is faring in the industry. For example, the specialty food industry as a whole might be experiencing record growth, but if you make teas and for some reason the tea market is struggling, it's good to know that up front. Try to get a handle on sales and trends within your subcategory in addition to understanding performance of the overall specialty food industry.

HYPERLOCAL MARKET

If you are initially focused on selling into local stores in your area, then you should also do a little research into how your local market is faring. Is the local economy growing or contracting? What is the demographic makeup of your city or county? Your local library is a great place to go to find a lot of this information; they have databases you can access for free. For those focused on the US market, the US census (www.census.gov) can also provide you with a tremendous amount of detail about specific areas based on the zip code or region you're interested in.

OUTLINING YOUR TARGET MARKET

Undoubtedly, some stores in your area simply have a certain cachet, and you'd love to get your products into them. They may be certain specialty stores, local chains, or a specific regional store that for you is the ultimate shelf you'd one day like to see your product on. The question is, are those ideal stores the same ones where your customers are shopping?

Before you spend the time, energy, and money to try to get your product into any store, you need to understand who your target market is and where and how they shop. While target market research is most often used in the planning and marketing stages of business development, any small food business that wants to get its products into retail stores needs to make sure that it's focusing wholesale efforts on the stores that appeal to its target customers. Not doing so means spending some of your very limited time and resources chasing after accounts that, in all likelihood, won't be sustainable. Even if you get your products into those key stores, if no one buys your products, your shelf space there won't last long.

So, who are your customers? Why would they buy your products—and *where* would they buy them? The more you know about your customers and their shopping habits, the better you can target the right stores and talk knowledgeably to buyers about why your products will appeal to their shoppers.

Ideally, comprehensive target market research occurred before you started your business (and is incorporated as a key component of your business and marketing strategies to this day). As a small business owner myself, though, I realize that things in the entrepreneurial world don't always happen the way they should. So, if you don't have current target market research at hand, take some time now to answer the following questions as best as you can:

- What type of person is buying your products (including online or in person purchases, or even customers who purchase from retailers you currently sell wholesale to)? For example, what is their age range? Are they married/partnered, single, or live with roommates? Do they have children and, if so, what are the age ranges of their children?

※ Why do you think they are buying your product? Is it a treat for themselves or their family after a long week, a healthy snack option, or a lifestyle choice due to health or personal concerns (i.e., vegan, gluten free, etc.)?

※ How do they feel about your price points? Do they question your prices before purchasing? Do you see a significant increase in orders or sales when you run a promotion that reduces your retail price point?

If you haven't been selling your products to consumers yet or don't have enough retail background to be able to answer these questions, use them as a guide as you draft a description of your ideal customer. Chances are, you've had this person in your mind all along as you've developed the product—in many cases, for specialty food products that are borne of an entrepreneur's passion, the ideal customer may be very similar to him- or herself.

Once you have a good idea of who your target market is, you need to find out where those people shop. This is the time to get boots on the ground and do some in-store visits to check out who's shopping there. Don't just drop by once and take a quick look around; go into the stores you believe your target market might shop in several times at different points in the day, the week, and even the month. The point of this is to watch shoppers to see who they are, what they're buying, and how they're making their buying decisions. For example, do they look at the ingredient panel of similar products before putting it in their carts? Do they compare price points of competing products? Or perhaps it's their kids who grab a favorite brand with the bright yellow packaging and put it in the cart without Mom or Dad objecting?

If you have a chance to develop a relationship with the store buyers (something that is often easier to accomplish at independent specialty stores than at supermarkets), take it. They are the best possible resource for understanding who shops at their stores. They are unlikely to have time to sit down with you one-on-one and give you an in-depth rundown of who their customers are, but you might be able to glean bits and pieces of useful information simply by talking to them and their staff.

As you do this research, you may find that certain stores you had initially been keen to get into simply don't attract the types of customers who would want to purchase your product. By the same token, there may be other stores that you weren't originally too excited about that rise to the top as you learn more about who shops there. In both cases, the research you do to identify your target market and understand where they shop can help you rank the stores. This way, you can spend your time and energy approaching the stores where your products stand the best chance of success—in not only getting onto the shelf, but staying there.

KNOWING WHO YOUR COMPETITORS ARE

With your understanding of who your target market is, now it's time to turn your attention outward and take a look at the competitive market. No matter how "new," "unique," or "hand-crafted" your products are, consumers have a limited amount of disposable income that they're willing to spend on specialty food products, and you need to understand how you stack up against your competitors. This information will help you to make strategic business decisions and to convey what makes your products different and better as you talk to buyers, brokers, distributors, and, ultimately, consumers themselves.

WHERE DO YOU FIT?

The first step in the competitive analysis is to determine where in the specialty foods industry you fit. Regardless of how novel your product is, you will need to be shelved somewhere—on the actual store shelves, but also in consumers' and buyers' minds. Are you a baked good, a frozen food, or a condiment? By understanding where you fit, you'll be able to make it clear to buyers what you are

Typical Food Categories

Baked goods/cookies/cakes

Baking ingredients

Condiments

Desserts/sugar/confectionery

Frozen foods

Meat/game

Pasta sauces/cooking sauces

Salsas/dips

Soups

Alcoholic beverages

Nonalcoholic cold beverages

Nonalcoholic hot beverages

Beverage mixes

Cheese/dairy products

Hors d'oeuvres

Pasta/rice/grain

Seafood

Spices/herbs/extracts

Chocolate/confectionery

Crackers

Jams/preserves/honey/nut butters

Oils/vinegars/salad dressing

Snack foods/chips

Food gifts

selling. This will also help you more quickly identify the right buyers for you to talk to within a store by ensuring that they make decisions for your category.

WHO ARE YOUR COMPETITORS?

You need to know everything you can about all competitors *within your category*. Don't list every competitor out there—only those who are directly competing with you for the same target audience. If you're hoping to get your products into independently owned health food stores, you probably shouldn't spend too much time worrying about what the brands on Walmart's shelves are doing unless you've seen those same brands at your local health food stores.

As you research your competitors, ask yourself the following questions:

- Who are your competitors? What are their brand names?

- What products does each competitor offer? (They might offer several similar products in different flavors.)

- How are their products packaged? In glass or plastic? Bags or boxes?

- What size packages do your competitors offer? If they offer several sizes, make note of that.

- What are the retail prices for each of their products and in their various sizes?

- Where in the stores are their products shelved?

- What types of stores carry your competitors' products? Are there significant retail price variations among different types of stores?

- Is your competitor a regional or local competitor, or is it distributed nationwide?

- Buy your competitors' products and taste them. Make as unbiased an opinion as possible and note how your products are similar and different.

- Take a look at competitors' packaging to see what product information is included on it as well as any product claims.

- How do your competitors market themselves in their advertising be it print, online, via social media, etc.? What is the "voice" of each brand?

- Do your competitors' products have attributes or qualities that yours don't, or vice versa? (If all your competing products have attributes that yours don't, ask yourself why and whether buyers and consumers are willing to accept a product without a given attribute.)

- Do your competitors regularly offer price discounts to consumers? If so, what do those discounts look like?

- What does your competitors' ingredient panel and nutritional analysis look like, and is there a significant difference from the ingredients or nutrients in your products?

> The online presence of competitors can provide you with a wealth of information. Take a look at their websites to see how they're positioning their companies, what sort of product claims they make, pictures of their products, and even a list of stores they sell through. Similarly, look through their Facebook, Twitter, Instagram, and other social media accounts, because all of this offers valuable insight into your competitors.

COMPARE YOURSELF TO YOUR COMPETITORS

After you have thoroughly investigated your competitors, it's time to figure out what makes you better, worse, or different. Buyers aren't interested in putting copycat products on their store shelves. What they want to know is how your product is different, and you're going to have to explain that to them. Similarly, understanding what makes your product different will help you develop packaging that can convey the differences to consumers. It's not an easy task to get a consumer who has been purchasing one type of product to switch over and try another company's unless it clearly and concisely conveys its benefits to them.

Use the following template to guide you as you do your competitive research. You may want to make additional copies of the blank template to accommodate a list of all of your competitors.

Competitor Evaluation

Brand Name/ Company Name	Products or Services Offered	Average Price Point	Marketing Attributes	Target Market	Perceived Strengths	Perceived Weaknesses

DEFINING YOUR UNIQUE SELLING POINT

You develop your "unique selling point" (USP) after you've compared your strengths and weaknesses with those of your competitors and have identified the top reason your target market would switch to your brand. The USP clearly conveys what makes you different from— and, ideally, better than—the competition. This is also going to be the number-one reason that buyers are willing to put you on their store shelves.

The USP combines what you already know about your target market and its needs with the benefits your product offers and why you'll be the best suited to fill the needs. One of the most often-used examples of great USPs is FedEx's classic slogan, "When it absolutely, positively, has to be there overnight." FedEx's target customers are businesses, so their USP is essentially a promise that important business documents, deliveries, and so on will arrive on time without any problems. That's a far cry from what one of their competitors, the United States Postal Service, promises (or, to be fair, what post offices in most countries promise).

So, as you look at all the information you've compiled, can you figure out what your unique selling point is?

Your unique selling point should (perhaps after several rewrites) be a concise statement no longer than a sentence. You want something easily explainable in advertising and in conversation with salespeople, brokers, buyers, and consumers.

> **Questions That Can Help You Develop Your Unique Selling Point**
>
> - Who's your target market, and what problems does it have? What needs does the market have that are not being met?
> - How do you solve the target market's problem?
> - What is your promise to the consumers in your market?

CHAPTER 4

MORE THAN JUST A PRETTY PACKAGE

THE SAYING GOES, "YOU EAT with your eyes first," and that's never been more true than in the specialty food arena. If your product packaging doesn't look good, you will never be able to convince a new consumer who has no history or experience with your product to pull it off the shelf and give it a try. In addition to trying to entice consumers and buyers, packaging also plays a critical regulatory role in ensuring that consumers get all the information required by federal and state laws.

Researchers estimate that the average consumer spends twenty seconds scanning a shelf. This means that you have just a fraction of that time to make your product jump out at shoppers and catch their attention. That's no simple task in today's crowded stores. With such limited time and attention spans—not to mention how many shoppers are also simultaneously on their smartphones or trying to keep their kids from running up and down the aisles—your packaging has to convey one key marketing message. Ideally this is your unique selling point about what makes your product not only different from, but also better than, your competitors'. Based on your research ensuring it resonates with your target market, you want that message or key attribute to sway shoppers into trying your product for the first time and to make your product easy enough to identify that they can find it again on store shelves. (If you've ever gone to the store looking for the product "with the bright yellow label" because you can't remember the brand name, then you know how important recognizable packaging is to consumers!)

> **Packaging Tip!**
> Knowing what resonates with your target market is the first step toward designing packaging that will help sell your products.

As in all good marketing, knowing who your target market is and what will resonate with it is important, but so too is having consistent brand identity. If you've already developed a look and feel for your company through a logo, preferred color palette, or even though your social media presence, then you want your packaging to have the same identity. There will be a disconnect with your audience if your brand packaging is fun and whimsical but your website is sophisticated and modern. You need to make sure that all visual elements of your marketing are aligned so that you're telling one coherent story, no matter how consumers find you.

When Designing Packaging, Keep in Mind...

WHAT YOUR COMPETITORS ARE DOING

Buyers and consumers will judge your products against other, similar products on store shelves, so you need to be sure you understand what your competitors are doing. Take the time to research how their products look on store shelves. Take note of the package sizes they use and what messages they're trying to convey with their packaging. For different categories of food products, packaging typically has an accepted "look" and size that are more or less consistent across the category. While you can certainly differ from the standard, you want to make sure that your packaging design doesn't confuse the consumer.

> Marge Granola, (www.margegranola.com) an artisan granola company, ran into issues when they first tried moving from farmers' markets to store shelves because their packaging looked smaller than that of competitors. Though the net weight of their products and their competitors' was the same, to shoppers it looked like they were getting less granola in Marge's packaging. With flat sales and their shelf space in jeopardy, Marge Granola revised their packaging to appear on par, size-wise, with their competitors'.

WHAT YOUR KEY STORES ARE SELLING

Spend some time visiting the types of stores you want to get your product into and see what the product packaging in those stores looks like. Packaging in high-end gift stores, for example, has a very different look and feel than product packaging found in typical supermarkets. You must create packaging that fits in at the types of stores you're most interested in.

IT'S BEST TO HIRE AN EXPERT

Packaging is so important that even for entrepreneurs on a tight budget, hiring a professional package designer is money well spent. Unless you (or a loved one) are a graphic design professional, you stand little chance of ensuring that your product packaging does your product justice if the packaging itself looks home-made. Even for products whose key attribute is being handmade, there is a big difference between a non-artist creating home-style packaging and the "authen-tic" home-style look done by a graphic designer. You can't expect consumers to trust your product—something they will put in their bodies—if the packaging looks subpar next to competitors'. Similarly, if getting your product onto store shelves and selling wholesale is one of your goals, buyers simply won't bring in your product if its packaging doesn't fit with a store's image and clientele.

USE STOCK

In the early stages of getting your business off the ground, use as much stock packaging as possible. Stock packaging is blank packaging you can buy to which you add your own labels, stickers, or tags. Not only is it cheaper to have items like stickers designed than a complete box or jar, you can also purchase stock packaging in lower quantities than what is typically required for complete, custom-designed packaging. This not only saves you storage space but is another way to save money until your business has grown enough for you to get custom-designed packaging of your own produced.

PACKAGING CONCERNS

When it comes to packaging, you have a wealth of options to choose from. Do you want your product encased in glass, plastic, a cellophane bag, a cardboard box, a tin can? This is just one of the hundreds of practical

> **"I Wish I Had..."**
>
> "Looking back, I see that one of the biggest mistakes I made was spending the money to have ten thousand custom-designed boxes printed. Not only did I have to pay for the boxes up front, but I then also had to find a place to store them. When you're just getting going, do you know how long it can take you to work through ten thousand boxes?
>
> Don't get me wrong, the packaging was beautiful. But if I had to do it over again, I would have used a stock box and created different, custom-designed sleeves with corresponding flavor information to go over it. That would have been significantly cheaper and much easier to store in the earlier days of my company!"
>
> ~ artisan food entrepreneur

packaging decisions you need to make as you consider how best to showcase your product.

Food Contact

It should go without saying that you want to make sure that when the consumer eats your product, it's as safe as it was when you made it. Therefore, any packaging that touches your product must meet FDA regulations for direct food contact. While not all stock packages meet FDA requirements, those that do advertise themselves as such. You can also ask a sales representative for more information.

Food Safety

If you plan to sell wholesale, where the product is not in your direct control the entire time until the consumer purchases it, you should take into account how you will keep your product safe. You may need to look for tamper-free packaging or ways to alert customers that your packaging has been broken into. Stickers that need to be ripped to gain access to the product is just one example of how you might be able to accomplish this.

Freshness and Spoilage

Depending on your product and your product's shelf life, you may need to look for packaging materials that help keep your product from going stale or potentially molding. If you are going to sell wholesale, you may want to include a "best by" date to your packaging so that consumers know when your product is out of date even if a retailer hasn't pulled it from the shelves. Remember that any bad experience a customer has with your product, even if it isn't your fault, is a reflection on your brand.

PACKAGING SIZES

Along with issues of food safety and spoilage, you also must determine what size package or packages your product will be sold in. There are four key factors you should keep in mind when making this decision:

Sales Channels

The way you package your product for sale at a farmers' market is very different from the way you would package it to sell it to specialty stores. And how you package it for specialty stores is different from how you package it for sale at Costco, as the latter is looking for bulk items whereas the former is more concerned with packaging presentation. Design your packaging according to the channels you're selling to and their needs. If you plan to sell wholesale, make sure that your products actually fit on retailers' shelves. For example, supermarkets tend to set all shelf heights for specific categories the same, so don't exceed normal shelf height.

Masterpack Containers

If you plan to sell your products wholesale, you won't just be selling one product at a time. You'll need to pack a number of products together into a larger box (typically known as masterpacks). Ideally, a minimum of twelve units of packaged product fits into one masterpack, which then acts as your minimum case quantity. Make sure that the products can be shipped undamaged within your Masterpacks.

Costs

As you evaluate different packaging sizes, keep in mind how different sizes change the cost—not only for you, but also for your customers, because each package holds more or less. For example, a two-pound package may appeal to you cost-wise, but the retail price point on a two-pound package may be too high for customers, keeping them from buying. An eight-ounce package might offer your customers a more reasonable price point.

Usage

Outside of selling to bulk stores like Costco and Sam's Clubs, if your package size is so large that the consumer won't need to buy the product frequently, it may benefit you less since this decreases the number of times you can connect with the consumer. And, if you're selling wholesale, it decreases turnover of your product from retailers' inventory. Additionally, you have to consider how different sizes of packaging and the rate at which consumers will use your product may impact the product itself. For example, unless someone is a very heavy user, it's unlikely that anyone goes through a thirty-two-ounce container of honey very rapidly. In the meantime, the honey may crystalize, leaving some consumers to think the product has gone bad—making them unwilling to buy from you again.

> **Tip!**
>
> As you look for packaging, talking with a graphic designer who is familiar with food packaging and/or working with sales representatives from companies that specialize in food packaging can help ensure that you're considering all aspects of this very important component of your product.

As you consider what type of packaging you want to use, don't forget to think about how much that packaging will cost to ship to you as well as how much it might cost to ship it, once filled with product, to consumers and retailers. Will the shipping cost be so exorbitant that it will turn buyers off? Packaging that looks great but is heavy to ship might not be your best bet if your business strategy involves shipping your products.

You should also think about *how* the product in your packaging will ship and whether the constant bump and bustle of getting from point A to point B will disturb the product at all. You want the product to arrive at its final destination looking just as good as when you packed it, so you should think about how the packaging itself will fare as well as how the product inside will do.

MORE ABOUT OUTER CONTAINERS

The outer containers that you use for shipping your Masterpacks and products should be made of corrugated cardboard that meets or exceeds a test weight of two hundred pounds. This means that the box can withstand up to two hundred pounds of weight placed on top of it without it collapsing and damaging the products inside. Remember, as you grow, you might start shipping your products to retailers by the pallet—so look for box sizes that not only fit all twelve (or more) of your minimum case quantity but that you can also easily fit onto a standard 40" x 48" pallet without any overhang. This will help protect your products during shipment. Shipping boxes, as well as other shipping supplies like packaging tape and packaging filler, can be found at office supply stores or at packaging sites like www.uline.com.

Your particular product may also need additional packaging elements such as dry ice to keep it safe during transit. In this case, it is worthwhile to talk to a packaging expert at UPS, FedEx, or another packaging and delivery company to find out what is required and the best way to ensure your product arrives safely.

CHAPTER 5

LABELING REQUIREMENTS FOR SMALL FOOD BUSINESSES

THIS CHAPTER CONTAINS THE MOST up-to-date labeling information for US food businesses as of its publication date. However, labeling regulations can and do change. Therefore, the following should not be construed as legal advice with regard to labeling regulations. Please consult with a qualified attorney and/or food labeling expert as needed.

The Food and Drug Administration (FDA) oversees food safety in the United States and ensures that it is properly labeled in almost all food products sold via interstate commerce, while the United States Department of Agriculture (USDA) is responsible for overseeing the safety of meat, poultry, and eggs that are sold across state lines. The labeling requirements are strict, and this book is not meant to act as a stand-in for proper legal advice. While I present an overview of some aspects of packaging and labeling that you should be aware of, it is your responsibility to ensure that your labels meet all requirements. More information about the FDA guidelines can be found at www.fda.gov.

SMALL BUSINESS EXEMPTION

The FDA exempts small businesses that gross less than $50,000 annually from food sales and $500,000 total sales annually (for all products, including food) from nutrition labeling requirements. So, if your gross food sales are over $50,000 but your total gross sales are less than $500,000 (even if all your company sells is food), you don't have to comply. The FDA requires small businesses to keep their own records—mainly tax filings—showing that they are exempt and to make them available to the FDA upon request.

Note that while your business may be exempt, it's worthwhile to consider the impact of not having nutritional labels may be perceived by retail buyers and on the psyche of the consumer. To them, your packaging may not look professional or "finished," and that may make them question the quality of the product inside. Some retail buyers may also require that you have nutrition labeling regardless of your FDA status. You need to determine, based on what you know about your consumers and your potential retail buyers, whether or not having nutritional labeling will impact their buying decisions.

NUTRITION LABELING AND EDUCATION ACT

The Nutrition Labeling and Education Act (NLEA), along with the Fair Packaging and Labeling Act, outlines the rules most US food companies must follow with regard to package labeling.

PRINCIPAL DISPLAY PANEL FACING

The principal display panel (PDP) is the part of the package that faces consumers when it's on store shelves. This panel must include the brand name, statement of identity (what the product is), and the net weight of the product (the product itself minus any packaging) listed in both metric and US customary system (i.e., in both grams, kilograms, or liters and ounces, pounds, or fluid ounces). The FDA has specific instructions on how each of these must appear on the package panel, including their font size restrictions, placements, and colors.

- The company's *brand name* is clearly shown on the front-facing panel.

- The *statement of identity*, which helps the customer understand what the product is (in these cases, rosemary and black pepper crackers and strawberry jam) uses common words that the public would understand. If a common description doesn't exist, then the statement of identity must be phrased in a way that is not misleading to the public.

- The *net quantity of contents* must be placed in the lower 30 percent of the packaging's visual area and be parallel to the base. It must contain both US customary measurements and metric measurements. The net quantity is only the measurement of the food weight (i.e., the net weight) and does not include the weight of the packaging.

Handcrafted Cracker Co.

ROSEMARY &
BLACK PEPPER
CRACKERS

Net weight: 6.2oz (175.76 grams)

Nutrition Facts
Serving Size 2 oz. (38g)
Servings Per Container Varied

Amount Per Serving
Calories 80 Calories from Fat 20
                        % Daily Value*
Total Fat 2g   3%
  Saturated Fat 1g   5%
Cholesterol 30mg   10%
Sodium 480mg   20%
Total Carbohydrate 15g   0%
  Dietary Fiber 4g   0%
  Sugars 10g
Protein 1g

Vitamin A 0%   •   Vitamin C 0%
Calcium 0%   •   Iron 0%

Percent Daily Values are based on a 2,000 calorie diet.

Ingredients: All-purpose flour, virgin olive oil, sugar, salt, rosemary, black pepper.

Manufactured by:
Handcrafted Cracker Co.
Milwaukee, WI 53212

DETERMINING THE AREA OF YOUR PRINCIPAL DISPLAY PANEL

It's important to determine the area measurement of your principal display panel since it impacts the font size you must use for your statement of identity and net quantity of contents information. A square or rectangular package can be measured by multiplying the height by the width, while cylindrical packaging should take the circumference of the packaging and multiply it by 40 percent of the packaging's height.

For the net quantity of contents, the smallest font you are allowed to use is based on the size of your packaging as measured above. The letters themselves must be measured by the height of a lowercase *o*.

PDP Size (in square inches)	Minimum Allowable Font Size
5 or less	1/16" (1.6 mm)
5–25	1/8" (3.2 mm)
25–100	3/16" (4.8 mm)
100–400	1/4" (6.4 mm)
400 or more	1/2" (12.7 mm)

ADDITIONAL RESTRICTIONS ON PACKAGING FONT

Fonts used on packaging must be easy to read and must be in a color that contrasts with the background. Artwork should also not crowd or obscure any of the required information on the principal display panel.

INFORMATION PANEL LABELING

The nutrition facts label, ingredient list, allergen list, and name and address of the producer are required to be placed together, without any interrupting artwork, on the first panel or space to the right of the principal display panel if the manufacturer has chosen not to include any of this information on the principal display panel itself.

NUTRITION LABEL

The FDA allows the nutrition label to be presented either vertically or horizontally on the packaging. However, specific rules apply to font size as well as the information that must be contained in the label. Therefore, it's advisable to work with a company that can provide an FDA-approved nutrition label in a JPEG format that you can add to your packaging.

Nutrition Facts Labels

Small Food Business offers affordable recipe analysis and nutrition facts labels for food entrepreneurs operating in the US and Canada. Visit www.smallfoodbiz.com for details.

INGREDIENT LIST

The ingredient list includes all ingredients used within the product from greatest weight to least. Additionally, if any of your ingredients is made up of other ingredients, those must be featured after the composed ingredient inside parentheses. For example, your chocolate chip cookies are made up of flour, sugar, butter, chocolate chips (sugar, chocolate, cocoa butter, milk fat, soy lecithin, natural flavors), eggs, and so on.

NAME AND ADDRESS OF THE MANUFACTURER, PACKER, OR DISTRIBUTOR

Your company name, city or town, state, and zip code is required on all packaging. If a company's address is not listed in a current copy of the city directory or phone book, the company's street address must also be included.

If you are not producing your own product (i.e., if you're using a copacker), then the label must also include the words "manufactured for" before your company name and address information.

LABELING EXAMPLES

Following are examples of information panel labeling for two different types of food packaging. Key aspects of the labeling include:

- The labeling information is located on the correct panel: to the right of the PDP.

- The nutrition facts label is present and includes a breakdown of the nutritional value of the food according to serving size.

✷ Both of these companies produce their own products and their street addresses are in local phone books, so their names, cities, states, and zip codes are featured on the panel as required.

✷ Note that both information panels are easy to read and are not crowded by artwork or other information, and the font is a color that contrasts with the background.

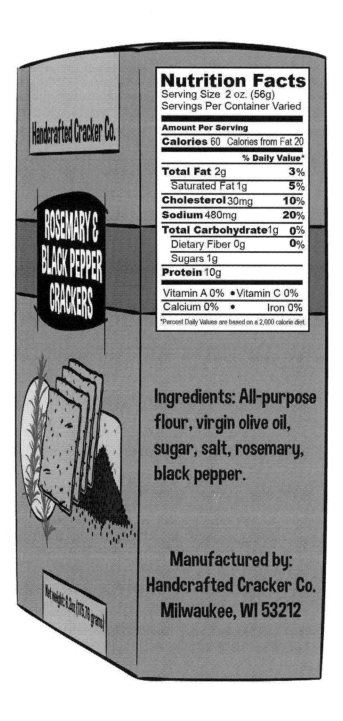

Handcrafted Cracker Co.

ROSEMARY &
BLACK PEPPER
CRACKERS

Net weight: 6.2oz (175.78 grams)

Nutrition Facts

Serving Size 2 oz. (56g)
Servings Per Container Varied

Amount Per Serving

Calories 60   Calories from Fat 20

% Daily Value*

Total Fat 2g	**3%**
Saturated Fat 1g	**5%**
Cholesterol 30mg	**10%**
Sodium 480mg	**20%**
Total Carbohydrate 1g	**0%**
Dietary Fiber 0g	**0%**
Sugars 1g	
Protein 10g	

Vitamin A 0% • Vitamin C 0%
Calcium 0%   •   Iron 0%

*Percent Daily Values are based on a 2,000 calorie diet.

Ingredients: All-purpose
flour, virgin olive oil,
sugar, salt, rosemary,
black pepper.

Manufactured by:
Handcrafted Cracker Co.
Milwaukee, WI 53212

Nutrition Facts
Serving Size 2 oz. (56g)
Servings Per Container Varied

Amount Per Serving

Calories 60   Calories from Fat 20

% Daily Value*

Total Fat 2g	3%
Saturated Fat 1g	5%
Cholesterol 30mg	10%
Sodium 480mg	20%
Total Carbohydrate 1g	0%
Dietary Fiber 0g	0%
Sugars 1g	
Protein 10g	

Vitamin A 0% • Vitamin C 0%
Calcium 0%   •   Iron 0%

*Percent Daily Values are based on a 2,000 calorie diet.

Ingredients: sugar, organic strawberries, pectin (dextrose, citric acid (assists gel), fruit pectin), lemon juice

Manufactured By:
Aunt B's Jams
Wilson, WY 83014

Jam

PRODUCT AND HEALTH CLAIMS: WHAT YOU CAN AND CAN'T SAY

We've all seen packaging with claims that eating the product will improve health. But what are you allowed to say, and what can't you say?

HEALTH CLAIMS

The FDA has determined that specific amounts of nutrients found in some foods are correlated with better health for specific health requirements. These findings are based on professional medical and scientific studies. Currently, claims include things like:

- Calcium and vitamin D affect osteoporosis

- Folic acid is important for fetal health

- Sodium affects hypertension

- Fat affects cancer

- Soluble fiber affects coronary heart disease

For a health claim about your product to be allowed on your packaging, your product must meet FDA guidelines for that specific health claim. For more details on the health claims that can be made, see

http://www.fda.gov/Food/IngredientsPackagingLabeling/LabelingNutrition/ucm2006876.htm.

Additional regulations pertain to calling a product "low fat," "sugar free," "cholesterol free," and the like. To use wording like this, products must meet FDA nutritional analysis guidelines. See

http://www.fda.gov/Food/GuidanceRegulation/GuidanceDocumentsRegulatoryInformation/LabelingNutrition/ucm064911.htm.

ORGANIC CLAIMS

In the United States, the term "organic" is regulated by the USDA, which oversees the National Organic Program. In combination with the Organic Foods Protection Act, these programs were put in place so that "organic" has a single, consistent definition. The National Organic Program labeling and marketing requirements apply to food businesses with gross revenue exceeding $5,000 per year from the sale of organic products.

For processed food products, at least 70 percent of the ingredients must be organic before one can say that the products are "made with organic ingredients." Even at the 70 percent level, though, the National Organic Program prohibits any food from using the term "organic" if the foods are produced using "excluded methods, sewage sludge, or ionizing radiation."

In addition, using organic ingredients is one thing—but getting certified by the USDA to be able to use the word "organic" (or the "USDA Organic" logo)—is another! If you sell more than $5000 of organic products in a year and want to use the organic term in your packaging or marketing, your organization must be USDA certified. This means that you must have an organic system plan that outlines the practices and monitoring you have in place to ensure that all "organic" products meet the required regulations. A certifying agent will likely need to visit your facility to check that you are following all rules before you can use any USDA Organic labeling.

If you can't afford to have your products certified organic or to use a minimum of 70 percent organic ingredients but still want to use organic ingredients, you can still call out which ingredients are organic in the ingredient panel. For example, your ingredient list might read: "Apples, organic cinnamon, water..." and so on.

More information about the National Organic Program can be found at http://www.ams.usda.gov/AMSv1.0/NOP.

GLUTEN-FREE CLAIMS

In 2013, the FDA outlined the requirements surrounding the use of the term "gluten-free" in food packaging and marketing. In the United States, in order to be considered gluten free, a product must have a level of less than twenty parts per million of gluten.

It's important to note that even if you make a product that contains no gluten ingredients, you must be careful of potential cross contamination especially when working within a shared or incubator kitchen setting or when working with a co-packer. It is possible to have your products tested for gluten content to ensure they meet FDA guidelines. Testing is available in food labs around the country; costs vary.

Currently, the FDA does not require a specific label design or wording, so products that meet all requirements may display the words "gluten free" or use a label of the company's own choice to alert consumers to the product's gluten-free status. Some food testing labs may provide gluten-free labels.

For more information about using the claim "gluten-free," see:

http://www.fda.gov/Food/GuidanceRegulartion/GuidanceDocuments RegulatoryInformation/Allergens/ucm362880.htm.

NON-GMO CLAIMS

Food made from genetically modified ingredients, either disclosed or undisclosed, has become a hot topic in the United States. Currently there is no legislation regarding the phrase "GMO free" in the United States, and to use it does not require testing. However, because of the ease of cross-contamination with GMO ingredients, one nonprofit, the Non-GMO Project, has devised a system that can test food for GMO ingredients. The Project developed a seal in 2013 for packaging that meets its standards. Please note that you cannot use this seal in any of your packaging or marketing unless your product has been verified by the Non-GMO Project to meet or exceed all of its standards.

For more information, see http://www.nongmoproject.org/product-verification/.

ALL-NATURAL AND NATURAL CLAIMS

"All-natural" and "natural" are among the hottest terms in the food world right now. It seems like every product is touting how natural it is. Interestingly, the use of "natural" (along with terms like "artisan," "handcrafted," and "handmade") is not regulated by the government other than very broadly that includes, among other things, that you don't process your food product with sewage sludge. Most people associate "natural" with food that is minimally processed, free of synthetic preservatives and additives, and free of artificial colors and flavors. The truth is, if you're making your food products by hand or via a small copacker (and choosing your ingredients with care), they are likely to fall under the broad category of what people think of as "natural."

Since there currently is no government oversight for this term, you can label and market your product as "natural." Be forewarned, though, that customers who value natural products are generally astute label readers (yes, this is a broad generalization), and there's no quicker way to lose customers than by marketing your product as natural if your ingredient list indicates otherwise.

KOSHER CLAIMS

For a product to be called or labeled "kosher" in any packaging or marketing, the product and the facility in which it is produced must undergo testing by a kosher certification organization. Simply using kosher ingredients in your products is not enough to call your product kosher, as there are myriad Talmudic rules that must be followed and verified by an expert first.

Because a qualified agent must often travel to your production facility, it may be best to search online for a kosher certification agency near you and contact it directly for more information.

UPC BARCODES

Packaging that "jumps off the shelf" takes many shapes and forms—it should fit the brand you've developed, offer the right color palette, and suit the stores you aim to get into. There's a whole host of things you need to take into consideration, but if you plan to sell your products wholesale, either now or in the future, then the most important part of your packaging is actually the most boring.

The UPC or barcode is a critical piece of your packaging that retail buyers want to see is in place prior to bringing your products onto their shelves. Independent specialty stores may not be as concerned about UPC barcodes, but if you target small chains or supermarkets at any point, they will be vitally important. Attention to this now can save you time and money that you won't have to invest in a packaging redesign down the road.

If you search online, you'll find a number of outfits selling discounted UPC codes. Don't buy them! Those low-cost codes don't really belong to you.

Take a look at the first set of digits in a barcode on any product you have nearby. This is called the "prefix." If you purchase from a low-cost barcode provider, this set of numbers won't be unique to you. For a company that plans to grow, you should own your own unique prefix. It acts as a company identifier in retailers' POS systems. The second set of digits changes with the product. For example, your peach salsa and your ghost pepper salsa both have UPC codes that start with "70989," but each salsa has its own secondary group of digits that follow those initial five numbers. This is key as you expand into supermarkets and start to work with distributors as they will program their equipment (scanners, registers, etc.) to reflect that all UPC codes beginning with that series of numbers belongs to your company. If you don't have your UPCs in place because you don't actually own your numbers, then you'll run into issues getting onto store shelves or getting distributors to carry your products because of the confusion and hassle this may create for them.

GS1 Company is the only legitimate source of UPC barcodes. It enables you to own the prefix and can provide you with additional UPC codes as you expand your product line. The initial application and setup cost does vary a bit depending on your business needs and there is an on-going annual licensing fee, but if you take into the account the cost of having to redesign and reprint packaging when you have to change UPC codes, you'll see that this up-front cost pales in comparison.

Visit GS1's website at http://www.gs1us org/get-started/im-new-to-gs1-us for more information.

EVALUATING YOUR PACKAGING CHECKLIST

- Does the packaging and product look good from four or five feet away (the average distance a consumer stands from store shelves)?

- Is it easily recognizable even at floor level or on the highest shelf at the supermarket? Chances are, new brands won't get ideal facings (at consumer eye level), so make sure your packaging stands out and can be recognized no matter where it is on the shelves.

- Does your packaging quickly and concisely tell consumers what your product is? Does it showcase the product's unique selling point (why the consumer should purchase your product over a competitor's)?

- Does your packaging fit with the overall branding of your other marketing efforts such as your website, your social media efforts, and everything else?

- Does your packaging fit, literally and figuratively, on the types of store shelves that you are most interested in getting onto?

- Does your packaging easily stand up (and not tip over) when on store shelves or displayed on tables?

- Is your packaging consistent with competitors' in regard to size and overall look?

- Have you tested the shipping of your products in this packaging?

- Does your product comply with applicable FDA direct food contact and labeling requirements?

- Do you know what your costs are for this product in this package size? Does the cost allow a reasonable MSRP?

CHAPTER 6

KEEPING UP WITH PRODUCTION

IT CAN BE EASY TO get caught up in wholesale dreams of high-dollar sales and brand recognition, but before you start talking to buyers, you should put some thought into determining how much product you can actually make. The last thing you want is buyers clamoring for your products and not being able to meet demand. Scarcity isn't necessarily a bad thing if buyers know in advance that they can only get your product during certain times of the year or that there's a limited supply to begin with. In fact, these can be marketing angles you can rely on to move product. But if a buyer has already ordered your product, chosen its place on the shelf (and the other brand that's getting bumped off) and is anticipating delivery, the store won't take too kindly to your sudden realization that you can't fill the order. You can only pull the apology routine so many times before buyers look elsewhere for product.

DETERMINING PRODUCTION CAPACITY

Let's say you're currently producing the product yourself in a kitchen. There are several considerations in determining your production capacity. To accurately determine this, the critical item is the great limiting factor that can hold you back.

The three biggest limiting factors food entrepreneurs run into are the availabilities of equipment, time, and money.

* *Equipment.* With your current equipment, how much product can you make per day (week, month)? Do you face potential limitations as your business grows? You product may need particular pieces of equipment like a mixer, ovens or stoves, or even pots and pans. The great limiter of your production may simply be size: large enough equipment to create the quantities you need. In an average operating day in the kitchen

building product inventory, how many individual product units can you physically produce?

🥄 *Time.* How much time does it take you to turn your raw ingredients into finished, packaged products? For example, account for *all* the time needed to bake, cook, and cool your products plus the time required to package it.

🥄 *Money.* If time and equipment aren't holding you back, money might. To produce product, you need capital to pay for ingredients, packaging, and perhaps staff and other production needs. Without access to enough money, you're limited to what you can currently afford to produce.

Thinking through these issues, you should be able to approximate how much product you can produce within a given period. With that information, you can reliably let buyers know at the time they place orders how soon you can deliver.

THE ROLE OF COPACKERS

You may work with a copacker (sometimes also called a contract packager) to manufacture and package your food products. The benefits of working with a copacker can include:

🥄 Freeing you and/or your staff to focus on the marketing and sales of your product. This can be especially beneficial if increasing production capacity on your own is too costly—or if you simply don't enjoy spending time in the kitchen (don't worry; this is actually fairly common. Day-in, day-out production is not nearly as exciting as product development.)

🥄 Limiting the size of your staff, which can reduce your employee costs

✼ Access to automation and equipment that increases production volume. This potentially also lowers your costs without a large capital investment in building a facility or purchasing new equipment.

✼ Potentially lowering your product unit cost. Copackers can typically buy ingredients in bulk at significantly lower costs than can stand-alone businesses.

✼ Taking the burden of overseeing production and complying with health regulations off your shoulders. The copacker manages these for its facility.

It's no secret to most people that many large manufacturers use copackers to produce their products, but many think that this isn't an option for a small food business. While copacking facilities that allow smaller minimum runs can be harder to find, they do exist, and more are popping up every day. In some cases, these copackers are companies that also produce their own product lines themselves and they're looking for a way to make money by allowing others to use their excess capacity. Finding these companies can take a little sleuthing on your part, but it's not impossible.

FINDING COPACKERS

Before you look for a copacker to talk to, you need to make sure you have a finalized idea of not only what type of product you want to make but also what sort of packaging is going to go into. Different copackers have the ability to produce different types of products (think,—for instance, dry mix versus salsa versus nutritional bar versus peanut butter, and so on, etc.) but each also have limitations on the type of packaging they can work with. If you aren't yet set on your packaging design or are open to making changes, (such as moving from a glass jar to a plastic jar for your product), then you might have an easier time finding suitable copackers.

Unless you have a recommendation from another food entrepreneur, your best bet is to start with an Internet search. Search on the term "copacker" along with your product type and location. Then make calls to facilities. Chances are that you don't yet need thousands of pallets of product, so ask about smaller minimum runs.

Small Food Business maintains a database of copackers who work with small producers. For more information, visit the smallfoodbiz.com site.

You may talk to more people who can't help you than who can, but ask even those who can't help you if they can suggest another person or facility you can talk to. Copackers often know others in the industry, so keep following leads until you find a potential fit.

Keep in mind that you aren't limited to the copackers in your backyard. While there are benefits to staying local, don't rule out those at a distance. With good communication and a good copacker, distance shouldn't be a problem.

WORKING WITH COPACKERS

Once you've identified several copackers you think might be good fits, talk with the managers and visit the facilities in person. Of course, it can take a lot of time and money to travel to distant facilities, but it's definitely worthwhile, because this is where your products—the products that you are spending time

When Danielle LiVolsi of NuttZo (www. gonuttzo.com) was looking for a copacker for her nut and seed butters, she contacted the Almond Association and the Peanut Council. Ingredient associations like this often have lists of copackers they can recommend.

and money to build customers' trust around—are going to be made. You want to know that your products are made safely and taste exactly as they do when you make them yourself.

In your conversations with copackers, you shouldn't hand over your recipes or any other confidential information until a nondisclosure agreement (NDA) has been signed. This is a confidentiality agreement between you and the copacker that prohibits the sharing of your proprietary information with any third party. Many copackers have NDAs already drafted that you can use, but I highly recommend that you work with a lawyer to either review such existing documents or draft one of your own to ensure that you and your proprietary information are well protected.

A very high level of trust is needed between you and the copacker, so don't hesitate to ask questions:

- Does the copacker pack any of your competitors' products? (If so, you may not want to use it.)

- What types of products does the facility already produce? Will your product(s) work with its existing machinery and/or staffing?

- Is the facility willing to work with your recipe?

- What is the minimum run order? (It could be a unit minimum or a production time minimum. Either way, ensure that you understand the structure and its associated costs.)

- Are there any packaging requirements or constraints? Will your current packaging (or the packaging you envision) work on their equipment?

- What is the production lead time? Does lead time increase or decrease dramatically at certain times of the year?

- Will you or will the copacker be responsible for ordering in ingredients? What if you have a specialty ingredient or want to work with vendors you've already identified? Where are the ingredients stored before they're used?

- Can the copacker warehouse and distribute the product for you? (In some cases this won't be an option and product is shipped to you on completion. But it never hurts to ask!)

- If the copacker doesn't warehouse, what is the cost to ship the completed, packaged product to you?

CHAPTER 7

PREPARING TO MAKE SALES CALLS

BEFORE YOU HEAD OUT TO meet with store buyers, you need to have your marketing material in order and your marketing pitch perfected.

SENDING OUT SAMPLES VERSUS MEETING IN PERSON

It is always better to meet buyers in person, either at the store or at a trade show, than to mail samples to them. Meeting in person builds relationships. You can ask questions that help you understand stores' business needs, and you can share your company's story. Just as customers connect strongly with a brand if they connect with the person behind it, so do buyers.

The reality, though, is that meeting with buyers is sometimes unrealistic. It may be too far or too expensive for you to travel, or buyers may simply not have the time to meet. In these instances, you should ask about how to submit products for consideration. Some stores want physical samples mailed—in that case, get the exact name of the person you should send to so your samples don't languish in some mail room for weeks. Others prefer information and photographs submitted electronically.

Whether you're meeting in person, mailing in samples, or submitting information electronically, find out when you can expect to hear back and don't be afraid to follow up if you haven't heard anything. Even a "we're

> **Product Casting Calls**
>
> Sometimes stores invite potential suppliers to meet on a specific day dedicated to evaluating their product mix. Though it may be daunting to be in a room with others competing for the same shelf space, this is a great opportunity to showcase your products and your company to buyers who might not otherwise be willing to meet in person. If such an opportunity presents itself, do what you can to go. Come prepared with product samples, your marketing material, and your well-rehearsed company story.

not interested" is a chance to learn about what you can do to better your odds with the next retailer you contact.

Marketing Material

YOUR MARKETING BROCHURE OR SALES SHEET

It's important to remember that buyers see hundreds, if not thousands, of new products every year. They are barraged with e-mails and phone calls from food entrepreneurs who want to meet with them, all eager to pitch their products and tell why they should be on that store's shelves. Do you think buyers will specifically remember your product and company name? Or do you think at some point, all those companies and products blend together in their minds? The latter is more likely.

Your marketing brochure, therefore, becomes your opportunity to quickly summarize what makes your company different, unique, and better than the rest. Marketing brochures come in all shapes and sizes, from one sheet of paper to a professionally designed catalog like the kind you receive in the mail. The size of the brochure itself is less important than what's inside it.

Keep these tips in mind as you design your marketing brochure:

- Your brochure is essentially the voice of your company, so be sure that it's professional. If you don't have strong graphic design skills, hire someone who can pull together a streamlined and professional document.

- You must include high-quality product pictures. They help remind buyers what your company offers and suggest how your product would look on their shelves. Don't forget that marketing brochures are sometimes filed away to be looked at again long after the samples have been eaten. Without your actual product right in front of the buyer, the brochure has to accurately display how great it looks. Again, hiring a professional can pay off in the long run, as quality images and good lighting help to make your product jump off the page.

‣ Include information about your company and your company's story. If your business is woman-owned, minority-owned, or you are a military veteran, you may want to indicate that. These designations can be very important to some buyers and may help you stand out among the competition.

‣ Similarly, if your product has any type of certification (e.g., it is gluten-free, organic, or fair trade), if you've won an award, or if you've been written up in popular consumer or business press outlets, call that out.

‣ If you have multiple product lines or flavors, showcase each individually using pictures plus short descriptions.

‣ Don't forget your contact information. You'd be surprised how many people forget to include crucial information like a company phone number, website, or e-mail address.

‣ Spend the money to print in color. Though it may seem expensive, a marketing brochure in color helps to show off your product and your company at its very best.

The following page shows an example of a one-page marketing brochure for a fictional company.

WOODEN SPOON SPICE

COMPANY BRINGING YOU A WORLD OF FLAVOR

Catch Me If You Cayanne A delicious blend of knock-your-socks off spices. Great for marinating steaks, chicken, or for anyone wanting to kick it up a notch on the spice index.

May I Mustard Seed Step away from the ordinary with this spice mix that provides just a hint of mustard seed hint. Goes superbly well on popcorn or with a good Reisling.

Nuts for Meg Our most popular holiday product, this spice mix will get the family round the table. Excellent in desserts, hot toddys, and for warm winter stews.

Cinnamon & Everything Nice A classic cinnamon and sugar mixture, the freshness of this cinnamon will pump up the flavor in everyday baking.

Pucker Up Paprika This spice mix brings the flavor of the South Indian continent to your table.

THE WHOLESALE ORDER FORM

Did you notice what wasn't included on the marketing brochure? Pricing, minimum order information, and special promotions. Ideally, you should create a marketing brochure that can be used again and again, as this will reduce your production and printing costs. Within that time frame, though, your prices or promotions may change. Including that information on a separate wholesale order form will allow you to easily make updates as needed. In addition to providing pricing and sales terms information, your wholesale order form does double duty, acting as the actual ordering form too.

To make it as easy as possible for a buyer to place an order by fax or by scanning and e-mailing, print your order form on a standard sheet of paper. The form doesn't have to be as well designed as the marketing brochure. Even the most graphically challenged can create a straightforward wholesale order form using any basic software program. Since the order form is less of a marketing piece than your marketing brochure, save a bit of money by printing it in black and white.

Be sure to include the following information on your wholesale order form:

> ### What About Online Wholesale Ordering?
> It is possible to create an online wholesale ordering section of your website and if you have the capability to do that you should as it will present the buyer with another purchasing option. That online wholesale page should be password protected so that only verified buyers gain access to your wholesale price list and can make purchases or place purchase orders and should contain other aspects of your marketing and wholesale pricing brochures such as product pictures, case sizes, and UPC information.

- A clear list of your products including the wholesale cost, the minimum order requirement, universal product code (UPC) number or other code (if applicable), the case weight (if your items are sold by a specific case quantity), and net weight.

- A description of your product's key selling points in short, concise sentences. Bullet points work well here, as the information is intended to remind buyers what makes your product different from your competitors'.

- Directions on how to place orders. Can a buyer fax in the order form, or should it be scanned and sent via e-mail? Do you offer online ordering via a secured website? Be sure to include your phone number, fax number, e-mail address, and website address as well.

- Payment terms: do you expect to be paid when the order is shipped, or do you allow net 15, net 30, or any other specific terms?

- Information regarding point-of-purchase material or display items available to the buyer as applicable.

The following is an example of the front and back of a wholesale order form for a fictional company.

Wooden Spoon Spice Company
Bringing You A World Of Flavor

Key Selling Points:
- We Work directly with certified fair trade spice farms around the world
- Ground fresh to order
- Available in bulk or 2 oz. sizes
- 100% All natural and low calorie recipes
- POS material is available to spark ideas and inspiration amongst customers

Terms:
- We Work directly with certified fair trade spice farms around the world
- Ground fresh to order
- Available in bulk or 2 oz. sizes
- 100% All natural and low calorie recipes
- POS material is available to spark ideas and inspiration amongst customers

Catch Me If You Cayanne

QTY	CASE	UNIT	DESCRIPTION	NET WT	UNIT UPC
___	$24	$2.00	2oz. bottled mix	2 oz	8-83422-0007-0
___	$85	$1.06/oz	Bulk mix	5 lbs	8-83422-0008-0

May I Mustard Seed

QTY	CASE	UNIT	DESCRIPTION	NET WT	UNIT UPC
___	$24	$2.00	2oz. bottled mix	2 oz	8-83422-0007-0
___	$85	$1.06/oz	Bulk mix	5 lbs	8-83422-0008-0

Nuts For Meg

QTY	CASE	UNIT	DESCRIPTION	NET WT	UNIT UPC
___	$24	$2.00	2oz. bottled mix	2 oz	8-83422-0007-0
___	$85	$1.06/oz	Bulk mix	5 lbs	8-83422-0008-0

Cinnamon & Everything Nice

QTY	CASE	UNIT	DESCRIPTION	NET WT	UNIT UPC
___	$24	$2.00	2oz. bottled mix	2 oz	8-83422-0007-0
___	$85	$1.06/oz	Bulk mix	5 lbs	8-83422-0008-0

Pucker Up Paprika

QTY	CASE	UNIT	DESCRIPTION	NET WT	UNIT UPC
___	$24	$2.00	2oz. bottled mix	2 oz	8-83422-0007-0
___	$85	$1.06/oz	Bulk mix	5 lbs	8-83422-0008-0

Fax or email this order form to sales@companyname.com. All orders will be confirmed. You may also contact (111)222-3456 for more information.
www.companyname.com

Wooden Spoon Spice Company
Bringing You A World Of Flavor

Key Selling Points:
- We Work directly with certified fair trade spice farms around the world
- Ground fresh to order
- Available in bulk or 2 oz. sizes
- 100% All natural and low calorie recipes
- POS material is available to spark ideas and inspiration amongst customers

Terms:
- Net terms are available with credit card on file
- To establish credit, please send three trade references, one bank reference, and your federal tax ID#
- Pricing is FOB Seattle, WA 98103
- There is a $25 fee on all returned checks

ORDER INFORMATION   DATE: __ / __ / __

SUBTOTAL: _____
SHIPPING: _____
TOTAL DUE: _____

ACCOUNT INFORMATION

Store Name: _____
Buyer Name: _____
 Alternate Contact: _____
Ship To Address: _____
City, State, Zip: _____
Phone: _____   Email: _____
Fax: _____   Website: _____

BILLING INFORMATION

Credit Card #: (Visa, MC, Amex):   Exp. Date: _____
Name on Card: _____
Billing Address: _____
City, State, Zip: _____
Signature: _____

Fax or email this order form to sales@companyname.com. All orders will be confirmed. You may also contact (111)222-3456 for more information.
www.companyname.com

TALKING TERMS: WILL YOU EXTEND CREDIT?

Earlier, we discussed the payment term "net"—an agreed-upon delay of payment to a specified date in the future. For example, "net 60" means that payment is due sixty days after an order is received. This delay of payment is essentially a credit extension that you provide to buyers.

Extending credit is fairly typical in the industry. If your cash flow can accommodate a delay between order fulfillment and payment, it is a benefit you can offer your retailers. That being said, small food businesses, many of which work under relatively tight cash constraints, typically ask the buyer for a credit card number to hold the order with. The business either charges the credit card on the agreed-upon date or relies on it as backup if another agreed-upon form of payment is not delivered on time.

Larger retailers may not be willing to provide you with a credit card for their orders; instead, they provide you with a purchase order and a letter of credit from a bank or another financial institution stating that the retailer is financially sound and has the means to pay.

This doesn't mean that extending credit is without risk. Almost every entrepreneur, at one point or another, is burned by extending credit to the wrong retailer. Even with a credit card securing the order, it is possible for the retailer to avoid paying by cancelling or even maxing out the card before you can charge it.

BEFORE YOU EXTEND CREDIT TO ANYONE

Determine the procedures by which you will extend credit—how long it is before payment is due and what the ramifications are of late payment. These might include an interest rate being charged on payments that are received late. These rates must stay below what is considered usury (i.e., they must not be significantly above accepted industry interest rates) and should be clearly conveyed to retailers prior to placement of an order.

While you hope it never happens to you, prevention is the best medicine. If you can, do credit checks on companies who are new to you or ask other entrepreneurs you know who work with those businesses if they can be relied upon to pay on time. Don't forget that every day they're late on paying you is another day when you don't have the money you need to run your business, so their negligence is a very real threat to your business.

Sadly, you should assume that you will run into one or two of these cases over the lifespan of your business. Develop a plan for how you will handle late payments. For example, you may want to call the company the first day that a payment is late. There's a very good chance, especially with independent specialty stores that are small businesses themselves, that payments innocently slipped their minds—or maybe they just need another day or two to be able to pay you. Trying to resolve the issue in a polite and professional manner is always the preferred way to go, as your goal is to get what is owed to you as soon as possible. After you get your money, you can decide whether or not you trust the buyer enough to do business with again. Possibly, you'll sell to them again but add the requirement that they pay up front for orders from then on.

Your plan should also include how you'll escalate contact to the store if you don't receive your payment by a specific day. This may even include sending a certified letter so that you're sure that they've received it. And, based on the applicable laws in your state, you should also outline in your plan when you'll take a client to court or hand a past-due invoice over to a collections agency (who will pay you a small portion of whatever they recover).

DEALING WITH BANKRUPT RETAILERS

Businesses fail for hundreds of different reasons, but if one of your retailers stumbles and declares bankruptcy before paying you, you'll be unable to collect on the debt until a bankruptcy court decides how the remaining assets of that business are to be divided among all its creditors. Depending on how much you're owed in such a case, you may want to ask a legal professional about trying to collect from a bankrupt client to recoup as much of what you're owed as possible.

CHAPTER 8

THE BENEFITS OF STAYING LOCAL

WHEN ASKED WHAT HIS OR her dreams are for the business, it's not uncommon for a specialty food producer to share visions of a product being carried coast-to-coast in major retail chains. Getting a brand into the big stores with nationwide reach is, many believe, the path to riches.

That may be true to a point, but the truth is that it takes a lot of time and money to achieve. Very few food products become overnight nationwide successes and have the production capacity to handle new demand without going broke. This doesn't mean you shouldn't strive for the prize, but in wholesaling, there is another path that entrepreneurs often overlook in their quest for big accounts...starting local.

In your own backyard, there are likely countless outlets where your product could be sold: local kitchen and gift boutiques, neighborhood grocery stores, and area coffee shops, to name just a few. While these may seem like small potatoes in comparison to getting in with a national store, building a strong local business base can do wonders to prepare your business, both operationally and financially, for that big national push down the road.

Before you discount the idea of focusing on your local stores first because your brand is destined for greatness, let me introduce you to Dave's Killer Bread. If you live in the Pacific Northwest, you may already know this story—but for those who aren't familiar, Dave's Killer Bread is a sliced sandwich bread company that, as of 2012, sold exclusively in the Washington and Oregon area. Their industry is so highly competitive that taking their products nationwide would have required a significant infusion of cash to support the type of marketing campaign necessary for a big product rollout.

Instead, this family-owned company stayed focused on producing the best bread the Pacific Northwest had to offer and supported their retailers by showcasing their products at farmers' markets and festivals throughout the region, giving customers the chance to talk one-on-one with Dave's Killer Bread employees and learn more about the brand and the story behind it. (The story is compelling: the "Dave" in Dave's Killer Bread is an ex-convict who turned his life around.)

This may all sound well and good, but the numbers are what really make this story jaw dropping. In 2012, Dave's Killer Bread sold a portion of the equity in their company for a reported *nine* figures. That bears repeating...they sold a portion of the company for a reported nine figures after focusing only on the Pacific Northwest market. If you don't think you can build a strong and financially successful business by focusing on your local market after hearing that story, then there's nothing else I can say that would change your mind!

WHAT EXACTLY DOES "LOCAL" MEAN?

"Local" is a bit of a loose term, and how "local" you stay really depends on where you live. But the idea is to open retail accounts with the stores closest to you that you can service on your own. Hyper-focus your attention on the stores in your neighborhood initially (say, within a ten-mile radius of your kitchen). As your business grows, move outward. Expand your radius to twenty miles, then fifty, and so on.

One manufacturer who spoke at a food conference mentioned that over the course of seven years, she was able to build her business into a multimillion-dollar brand by using this approach—never going more than a hundred miles from her kitchen. Her rationale, as we'll talk more about in a minute, was that she wanted to build relationships with retailers and service those accounts herself. She didn't want to hand that over to brokers or distributors because she believed that no one would sell the product as passionately as she would: no one believed in it as much as she did.

LOCAL MEANS DIRECT SELLING

From a financial standpoint, staying local and working with retailers in your geographic area means that you can hit the streets yourself. By selling direct, you not only save on broker and distributor fees (which means more money to put back into your business), but you also learn what marketing messages resonate with buyers and which fall flat. Remember, no one will ever be as passionate about your product as you are, so staying local and selling direct allows you to hone your sales skills and share your passion with buyers.

LOCAL GIVES YOU A CHANCE

Without a doubt, you can do everything right and still struggle to get your products onto store shelves. It's a crowded marketplace, and buyers want to know that every inch of shelf space they have will be profitable for them. This is especially true for national stores where the buyers are evaluated on the success of products in the category they're responsible for.

While buyers for smaller, independent stores are just as concerned with having profitable products on their shelves, they also want something different—something that is not available everywhere else—so that customers have a reason to come in and shop with them. New, unique products like yours are what keep local, independent buyers interested—for the very reason that your products aren't available at every supermarket. Being able to offer products that are different from what the big retailers carry is important to local retailers; therefore, they're more willing to take a shot on a new company like yours.

By the same token, local stores that carry specialty items also usually have a higher price point, and the customers in those stores are used to paying a premium for unique products. This means that if you get on your local store's shelf, your higher-priced, high-quality product won't be sitting next to a similar but mass-manufactured product that retails for half the cost.

LOCAL GIVES YOU A CHANCE TO BUILD RELATIONSHIPS WITH RETAILERS

One of the biggest benefits of starting local is that it gives you a chance to physically go out and meet with buyers from your local stores and get to know them. Buyers who you only talk to on the phone or via e-mail simply don't have the same type of connection to you as buyers you see face-to-face in meetings. This not only gives your product a far greater chance of getting shelf space, but as you build these relationships, the buyers can provide you with insight about how your products are performing on the shelf. This is critical insight for growing and modifying your business.

As an example, a small, Asian-inspired ice cream company approached several major supermarkets but was turned away in every meeting. Meeting with a buyer for a local store revealed that the company's margins weren't in line with industry norms, resulting in a smaller return-on-investment for the stores than with competitive ice cream products. With that one piece of information, the producer was able to go back to the drawing board, changing out some ingredients to bring the price point down to a level that would provide stores with the margins they needed. Not only were stores more interested, but investors expressed interest in the company too, thanks to the sales the company was generating. Had this producer not had the relationship with the local buyer, it might have kept on knocking on doors without success.

LOCAL GIVES YOU A CHANCE TO SEE WHAT'S WORKING

Once your product is on a few store shelves, you can use them as a test market to see if your product is drawing in customers as you've anticipated. While you can't physically be in the retail stores every day watching over every customer, your relationship with the store buyers can give you great insight into how customers react to your product and what questions they ask. This might result in changes to your marketing strategy or packaging design, or perhaps it'll encourage you to add new flavors that customers are asking for. In any case, the more information you can get, the better prepared you'll be when you do have a chance to get in front of national buyers.

LOCAL GIVES YOU A CHANCE TO MAKE MISTAKES (AND RECOVER FROM THEM!)

It's a fact of entrepreneurship that no matter how well you prepare or how thorough your business plan is, you're going to make mistakes. Buyers for large retail chains (or even many large distributors, for that matter) with whom you don't have a strong relationship have little tolerance for mistakes that end up costing them money. A local buyer, however, especially one for an independent specialty store, is more willing to be lenient about the fact that you're still learning the ropes and growing. They are typically more understanding and more willing to keep your product on stores shelves rather than cut your product immediately and refusing to take your calls again (as often happens at larger stores). They know that their small suppliers may make some mistakes.

LOCAL GIVES YOU THE CHANCE TO GROW SALES ON YOUR OWN

In chapter 1, we discussed how brokers and distributors can help you grow your business by opening up new accounts for you. We also mentioned, though, that brokers and distributors expect to be paid for their time and effort—and that is money coming out of your pocket. As a small business, that's money you could probably put to use elsewhere for growth. Staying local, building relationships with buyers on your own, and selling direct enables you to keep all of the profit between the cost of making the product and your wholesale price. That's money you can use to grow your business...or even pay yourself every once in a while.

> One food artisan, in an effort to keep as much cash in her business in the beginning as possible, treated herself as a food broker for the first few years. Rather than take a regular paycheck, she gave herself a "commission" from every order she received, which is not unlike how a food broker works. She says this helped motivate her to get out and sell (something that was not her favorite business task in the first place), and it kept most of the revenue in the business instead of tied up in payroll.

LOCAL GIVES YOU THE CHANCE TO GROW OPERATIONALLY

As tempting as it may be to go after those big accounts, in a product-oriented business like the food industry, it means you have to fulfill orders. A big order can mean big trouble if you don't have the production capacity in place to meet it. You may want that million-dollar order, but do you know how you'd actually fill it if you received it right now? We've already noted that nothing will cause a big account to drop you quicker than if you don't fulfill an order on time!

Starting with local stores, even though they may place smaller orders, enables you to ramp up your production over time. As you grow, you may realize that certain pieces of equipment are critical for larger-scale production, and if you stay local at first, you'll have the time to find the right pieces to purchase or to find the right copacker who can assist you with production as your business gets more and more orders.

CHAPTER 9

WORKING WITH FOOD BROKERS

FOOD BROKERS, AS WE'VE DISCUSSED, are independent sales representatives or independent sales companies that assist you in getting your products onto store shelves. They take your products (and those of the other brands they represent) to stores with which they have established relationships. To the store buyer, the benefit is that they can do "one-stop shopping" with the broker, placing an order for multiple products through one point of contact.

Brokers are not limited to working solely with store buyers. Some have relationships with distributors who might be able to make your product more widely available to consumers. Don't feel, however, that you can only work with brokers or distributors. Many successful food entrepreneurs work with a combination of brokers and distributors while making their own in-house sales calls on certain accounts.

It's important to remember that while brokers make sales calls to open new accounts and solicit reorders for you, they don't actually facilitate order fulfillment. Brokers don't purchase inventory from you, so when they receive an order from a buyer, they pass it along to you to fill and ship.

As previously mentioned, brokers are typically paid by an agreed-upon commission as a percentage of each sale for the sales service they provide. The broker is therefore incentivized to get out there and sell your product. It's worth noting though that since brokers have a number of different brands in their portfolios, they tend to spend the most time and attention on their top-selling brands since this has the greatest positive impact on their incomes. This means that a broker may not be willing to take on your products or may jettison or pay less attention to them if they are slower to sell. While this can unnerve some entrepreneurs, the upside is that most brokers want to present buyers with new and unique products, so hopefully they'll give your brand a fair shot. Return to chapter 2 to review how food brokers make money and how to price your products appropriately.

HOW A GOOD RELATIONSHIP WITH A GOOD FOOD BROKER CAN HELP YOU

A good food broker can help you understand your market and industry better. Because food brokers are out in the field most of the time and attend industry trade shows, they have access to information that you don't. A good broker will share it with you.

You'll also get strategic advice. Due to brokers' breadth of experience and insight, they can be an excellent source of advice and feedback. Brokers can also be marketing partners. As you develop retailer promotions (see the "Supporting Your Retailers" chapter), a food broker can give you ideas on what works best for retailers based on the daily interaction they have with buyers. They can help guide your promotions and in some cases may be called upon to put the promotions into effect with retailers. They can also suggest what type of point-of-purchase material you should have to help capture consumers' attention at the stores.

Brokers can be your product advocates with buyers. Granted, food brokers represent multiple products, but if a retailer has expressed interest in yours, a good food broker will do everything possible to make sure it stays on that store's shelves. This might include advocating a high-profile location for your product within the store, merchandising your product with other, complementary products to increase impulse buys, or even straightening the shelves when they're in the store to make sure that your product always looks its best.

Brokers can help you sell more stuff! At the crux of it, the goal of a good broker is to sell more products, since they make more commission that way. This means that hopefully, they are out there selling more of your products for you. Ideally, a good broker can sell more products into more stores quicker than you can on your own. This frees you up to work on other aspects of your business, confident that your products and your brand are well represented out in the marketplace by a broker you trust.

FINDING FOOD BROKERS TO WORK WITH

There are hundreds of food brokers out there. Some have been in the business more than thirty years, and others are just starting out. As with any kind of salesperson, there are good brokers and not-so-good ones, so the best place to start finding one is to ask other specialty food businesses if they have someone they use and trust. You might also try asking any buyers with whom you have a close relationship and see if there are brokers they respect.

Otherwise, food-specific trade shows are great places to find brokers. If you're exhibiting, you can usually count on brokers walking the show floor. If they're interested in your products, they will approach you. Last, when in doubt, the Internet is a great (if not overwhelming) resource. Type in parameters (like "food broker natural products Pacific Northwest") and see what pops up.

> Small Food Business maintains a database of food brokers who work with small food brands at www.smallfoodbiz.com.

There are countless food brokers out there and, as in all industries, there are those who excel and those who don't add much value to the businesses they work with. Brokers may approach you or you may seek them out, but no matter how you come into contact, you should look for these characteristics:

- *Good communication.* A good food broker will not just represent your products to potential buyers but also have a finger on the pulse of the specialty food world. He or she should be able to provide you with industry information on trends and give you feedback from buyers.

- *Trustworthiness.* Never forget that when you hire a food broker, you are hiring someone else to represent your brand. The store buyer may never meet you in person, so the only personal connection they'll have to your brand is through the broker. Is this person someone you want representing your brand? Do you think he or she understands and can convey your marketing message?

Experience. Experience and contacts in this industry count, but that shouldn't scare you off from someone new to the field. Food brokers who have been in the industry for a long time often don't have room in their portfolios for new lines or have such mammoth brands as clients that they don't have time or incentive to dedicate much attention to your brand. On the flip side, someone new may lack the industry contacts necessary to open up big accounts but may be more willing to take on new brands and be "hungrier" to make a name for him- or herself. You need to find the balance that you're comfortable with.

Accounts. As mentioned, contacts in this industry are important, and you want a buyer who has contacts in and relationships with stores that you're aiming to get into. Ask prospective food brokers what their top accounts are and see if they fit with your goals. The key word here is *goals*. It's easy to get swayed by a food broker who has contacts at Whole Foods Market, Kroger, and other national chains, but if your business isn't at the point that you're ready to take on such accounts or it's simply not where you see your brand sitting, you can't be afraid to say no (or "can we talk again later after my business has grown a little bit more") if it doesn't seem right for you.

Competition. It's worthwhile to ask the broker what competing brands she or he carries. Do you want to be represented by a broker who also represents some of your competition? In some cases, you might, since the contrast could help your product stand out all the more. On the other hand, showcasing your products next to a competitor's—especially one with a significantly lower price point—may result in buyers opting for the other product.

Specialization. Does this food broker specialize in specialty foods, or does she or he represent a wide range of brands including mass-manufactured products? While the majority of mass-manufactured products are sold via distributors these days, you may prefer a food broker who is committed to selling specialty food and can speak with confidence to its differences from and benefits over mass-manufactured food.

🥄 *Channels and region.* Some food brokers specialize in certain geographic regions or specific channels, such as selling only to gift stores or health food stores or drugstores. Your product type and brand style may simply fit better in one channel than another, or you may have shipping concerns for your product (for example, shipping your chocolates across the country in the height of summer may not be something you're ready to tackle just yet). Therefore, look for brokers who focus on the stores or regions that are the best fit for your products and your company.

🥄 *Promotions.* A good food broker is willing to help you implement promotions and can suggest others that might work. (We'll discuss promotions that can help sell more products in chapter 16.)

You should also be frank with food brokers about what you hope to achieve through the relationship. Ask them if they believe they can help you get there and how they plan on doing it. And always, regardless of what a broker tells you, call the references the food broker or brokerage company provides to find out about their experiences and relationship with the broker.

> Working with a broker means you're putting your trust in another person and your brand in someone else's hands. Try to meet with brokers in person—or, at the very least, via Skype or Google+ or FaceTime, etc.—to see if they pass the "gut check" and appear to be a good fit for your company.

SETTING THE TERMS OF YOUR WORKING RELATIONSHIP

You've narrowed down your list of prospective food brokers to the top contenders, but before you go too much further, you need to create a written contract to be sure that you and the broker are on the same page. As do some of the other service vendors we've mentioned, many established food brokers have stock contracts available, but as always, read it thoroughly and consult with an attorney as needed. You're never automatically bound to everything presented in a contract; you can negotiate for changes to them before you sign. Don't be afraid to negotiate hard for yourself and your company,

Whether you modify an existing contract or create one with an attorney, it should include the following points:

- An outline of exactly which products the food broker will represent. Is it your full product line or a sub segment?

- The geographic regions and types of stores the broker works in. Brokers often ask for exclusivity to a region or specific type of store. Since this prohibits you from working with other brokers in the same area, your contract should explicitly state the channel and geographic boundaries yours will be working within. When it doubt, always be more specific—"the Pacific Northwest" is a large and less definite region than "the state of Washington" or "a one-hundred-mile radius around Seattle."

- Set a time frame for when the contract is valid. Include a start and end date, what is expected in terms of performance, and what the procedures are for terminating the relationship (i.e., you will give the broker thirty days' notice, etc.)

- How much the broker will be paid and how often they'll invoice you. Will you work on a cash accounting basis (you only pay the broker for orders after the retailer has paid you)? Or will you be working on an accrual basis (you pay the broker when the invoice is due whether or not you have received payment yet from the retailer). This is important to think about, because so many retailers you sell to may ask for net terms in which you agree to wait for payment up to thirty, sixty, or even ninety days.

🥄 Similarly, outline exactly what terms the broker may extend to retailers as well as procedures for opening up new accounts.

🥄 What action the broker must take on unpaid retailer invoices. This is especially critical when working with brokers who call on distant accounts that you cannot collect payment from in person if need be. In those situations, you'll need the broker's help to collect payment, so you need to agree on how many times you'll contact a client for payment and, if that doesn't lead to a resolution, what steps you'd like the broker to take.

🥄 How new orders will be transmitted to you. What lead time do you expect to need during busy periods? Make sure that you and the broker are in agreement about both of these.

🥄 Information about any "house accounts" you already have. These are accounts that you've already opened that may fall within the broker's territory. You don't want to pay the broker a commission on sales where you are the one maintaining the store relationship. Alternatively, however, if you want the broker to take over the reins on accounts you've opened and you'll pay for that service, make that clear.

🥄 How you prefer to be communicated with (some prefer e-mail, the phone, or Skype, for instance), how often, and what sort of feedback you want. Remember, brokers are the ones out there showing your products to retailers, so they'll probably hear both good and bad about your products—this is all information you can use to create better packaging, revise your marketing,

Joint Sales Calls

Like most people, sometimes buyers want to see the face behind the brand—meaning they want to meet you! This is actually a great opportunity to share your personality and story with retailers and help build a strong connection between them and your brand. This can be especially key if yours is a new brand the broker is carrying or you have a new product to introduce. See if your broker is open to making joint sales calls with you occasionally. This doesn't necessarily mean you have to fly all over the country. Just take advantage of trips you already have planned for trade shows or vacations and extend them by a day or two for joint sales calls if you have a broker in the region.

or help you decide which new products to release next. You should also specify how you will submit product information to the broker as well as how many samples, sales sheets, and other materials you're expected to provide, and when or how often the broker would like to receive these. Communication with your broker is key to a successful relationship.

ADVICE FROM FOOD BROKERS ABOUT WORKING WITH FOOD BROKERS

The most successful business relationships between brokers and food entrepreneurs are those where both parties work to benefit each other. Here are some thoughts from food brokers on how food businesses can help build and maintain successful relationships:

The producer needs to clearly understand what role brokers play in the business and set expectations accordingly. So, what do brokers do? Brokers help to develop new business. Brokers help to drive ongoing sales. The key word is "help." Ultimately, this is the producer's business. The producer should not simply hire a broker and think, "Whew, that base is covered. Now I can forget about sales." That's a recipe for disaster.

The producer should not disappear once a broker is hired. The producer should make him- or herself available for important sales calls. Often, closing new business or deepening existing relationships is much easier when the producer is present. Just the simple act of showing up demonstrates a commitment to the business. Producers should also expect to spend time in key retail stores as well meet with store personnel and/or doing product demos—especially early on. "Meet the producer" events are big in retail food marketing these days.

The precise roles that brokers play depends on what the entrepreneur brings to the table besides a great product. At one end of the spectrum, a broker could be hired to execute a well-defined and market-tested sales plan. At the other end of the spectrum, a broker could be hired to create the plan from scratch and then execute it—acting like a vice president of sales. The right role for the broker depends on the expertise and maturity of the entrepreneur. The first model is well suited for a company that has been in business for a few years and has achieved solid year-over-year growth in a specific region. It has a solid sales plan and a solid marketing plan. This company may be seeking a broker as it sets about expanding into new territories. The second model is well suited for a young small business with a passionate owner with limited experience. In this case, the owner may call upon the broker's expertise and experience to fill in some of the their own gaps. Food business owners must honestly reflect upon what they bring to the table and what their needs are. Once that is understood, then s/he must assess how well a broker candidate fits. A large national brokerage probably wouldn't be a good fit for a young company that has a passionate owner with limited experience. A stand-alone broker may not be the best fit for a business with a successful formula that is seeking to go national in the most efficient way possible.

The artisan entrepreneur must not forget about marketing. Brokers help to get products into stores. Brokers help to position the product within the store and meet with store personnel, but marketing builds the brand. Marketing includes advertising, demos, promotion, and more. Entrepreneurs need to develop a marketing plan including a budget. It may be advantageous for the owner to work with the broker on the marketing plan and budget, especially if the owner has limited experience in this area.

CHAPTER 10

WORKING WITH DISTRIBUTORS

IF YOUR AIM IS TO get your products onto the shelves of supermarket chains, convenience stores, and/or big-box retailers, then you will most likely need to work with distributors. In large part, the arrangement is driven by the fact that these stores are very concerned about store security; by working with only a handful of distributors, they know who is going in and out of the backs of their stores. Additionally, it's far easier for these stores, which may carry thousands of products, to work with only a few points of contact for ordering and invoicing rather than try to manage independent relationships with individual suppliers. Even if a category manager from one of these stores meets with you one-on-one and likes your product, you may still need to work with a distributor of the store's choosing to actually get your products onto the shelves.

Distributors, however, are not in the business of convincing retailers to bring on new products—that is more the realm of brokers and your own sales team. Where distributors shine is on the logistics end. Like brokers, distributors have selections of products they represent, but unlike brokers, distributors actually purchase inventory from you and store it in their warehouses. They then oversee the holdings until they sell to one or more of their clients. Then they coordinate the transportation logistics of moving inventory to the stores.

Spend any amount of time in the specialty food industry, and you'll soon find that any mention of distributors can evoke very different reactions. Some entrepreneurs absolutely love working with distributors, as there are some incredible benefits to it. But at the same time, there are things to be cautious of before you enter into an agreement with a distributor.

PROS OF WORKING WITH DISTRIBUTORS

The right distributor (or distributors) can help you rapidly grow your business because the entire goal is to move large quantities of product into stores. Keep in mind that you must have the production capacity to meet growing orders before you start working with a distributor.

Even though you'll make less money per item (because you sell to distributors below your wholesale price, as we noted in chapter 2), a good distributor helps you make more money in the long term. Their orders are for larger quantities than orders by individual stores; this might enable you to lower the cost of your production. Similarly, distributors like to keep several weeks' worth of inventory on hand, which enables you to plan your production schedule accordingly.

Since distributors commonly oversee the transportation of the order from you to their warehouses and then on to the customer, it can save you money and time. You won't have to coordinate shipping to multiple retailers. That's resources you can put to use in other areas of your business.

Speaking of transportation, some products need the logistical expertise of a distributor so they can reach a wider audience. This is especially true for frozen products like ice cream or popsicles, which can't be easily shipped across the country without an investment in your own refrigerated trucks. The right distributors already have those trucks—or relationships with refrigerated trucking companies—and can take that logistics headache away from you.

Some retailers choose to work with distributors because of additional services the distributor provides—such as stocking the shelves, changing out any pricing, and helping to implement promotions. Distributors also act as intermediaries between food companies and retailers: retailers don't need to try tracking down suppliers separately when they have questions. Instead, they ask the distributors to get answers for them. Similarly, the retailers' accounting departments don't have the hassle of paying hundreds or thousands of checks. They can just send the distributor one check that covers all the various products they've ordered. In fact, this time and cost savings for the retailer, combined with the minimization of potential loss or theft of products, is why many larger stores will only work through distributors to order products and stock their shelves.

CONS OF WORKING WITH DISTRIBUTORS

Not surprisingly, everything is not perfect in distributor-land, especially from the standpoint of a product producer. Because distributors have so many products in their portfolios, they don't spend a lot of time actively selling retailers on new brands unless they have a large incentive to do so. Therefore, if you work with distributors, you'll need a strategy for getting your products in front of retailers. One way might be to participate in distributor trade shows, where distributors encourage their vendors to set up booths (for a cost) and invite retailers to walk the aisles.

With distributors mediating the relationship between you and the chosen retailers, you may not get as much feedback about your product and its performance relative to competing products like you would from a broker or a store buyer you work with directly. In fact, you may not even have a complete list of all the stores where your products are sold and won't know if certain products or flavors sell better in some stores or regions than in others. Working directly with buyers, you get all of this information and can make marketing decisions based on it. Some distributors will help pull point-of-sale data that shows how your product is performing, but you can't always count on this. You may even have to pay an additional fee for this, which can make it hard to develop an impactful marketing strategy. Even after you've decided on a marketing strategy, you might have to pay extra for enacting a promotion or offering point-of-purchase material.

As you can see, it would be foolish to start working with a distributor assuming that your only cost is the margin you're giving up via distributor pricing. There are hundreds of ways distributors seek to make money from their vendors, and you need to be prepared to understand and pay those fees. But you also shouldn't be afraid to stand up and question any fees that seem confusing or suspect.

HOW TO KNOW WHEN YOU'RE READY FOR DISTRIBUTORS

None of the above is meant to scare you away from distributors by any means. At a certain point, as you look to gain shelf space on major retail chains, distributors are likely to be your only avenue onto those shelves. However, many food entrepreneurs make the mistake of trying to work with a distributor too early in their lifecycles, and that can be a costly mistake. Make sure you're ready to dive into a distributor relationship by asking yourself the following questions:

- Do I have the capability to ramp up production to fill large distributor orders?

- Do I have the funds to ramp up production, including hiring staff and purchasing additional ingredients or packaging, that might be needed to work with distributors?

- Am I targeting stores that require working with a distributor?

- Have I built out my distributor price point? Does the margin allow for funding other aspects of my business (such as administrative costs and marketing expenses)?

HOW TO FIND DISTRIBUTORS TO WORK WITH

Say you've answered yes to the above questions and are eager to start finding distributors. The best way to find the right distributors for you to work with is to start by asking your target stores who they work with. Not every retailer works with every distributor. If your choice retailer has a list of several it works with, contact those distributors for meetings. (By the way, don't worry if you had some "no" to some of the earlier *Are You Ready* questions. Just because you say no today doesn't mean you're saying no forever. As your business grows, you can always revisit the idea of working with distributors.

It's far better to work with them when you're ready than try to jump in too early and potentially get burned!)

You might also try talking to other small food manufacturers like yourself and ask for distributor recommendations. This can work in your favor, as the small producers might be willing to introduce you to the right individuals within the company. Plus, these distributors have proven they understand how to work with smaller companies like yours.

Distributors also flock to industry trade shows on the lookout for new products and brands. Being an exhibitor at trade shows is a great way to get your products in front of them. If that doesn't yield the results you were hoping for, purchase the trade show's list after the show if it's available and contact the distributors individually to see if you can meet with them.

Trade shows can also be beneficial if you've already highlighted some distributors you think might be good fits for your company but you don't have the funds to travel around the country to meet with them. You can contact the distributors before the show and let them know you'll be vending at a booth or walking the show floor and can meet while you're there. Keep in mind that the large industry trade shows are the Super Bowl for distributors. They'll be meeting with their key retailers and suppliers while they're there, so you need to contact them well in advance if you're trying to squeeze onto their schedules. Be very respectful of their time. More information about exhibiting at trade shows can be found in chapter 17.

> **Is a National Distributor Better Than a Regional One?**
>
> Actually, a national distributor is not necessarily better; it all comes down to what your business goals are. A national distributor might not focus on smaller regional chains that could prove to be very profitable to you, and they may charge higher promotional fees. On the flip side, a national distributor might be able to help get you into every store in a big chain regardless of its own location whereas a regional distributor typically only focuses on stores in its area. Keep in mind, though, that you might get better customer service and more attention to your products with a smaller regional distributor.

GETTING SIGNED ON WITH DISTRIBUTORS

Once you've narrowed down the list of distributors you think you would like to work with, you should contact each organization for directions on how to proceed. It's not uncommon for new vendors to be asked to make a sales presentation to the distributor's purchasing team. Essentially, this is an audition for your company and your products. The distributor will determine whether or not you make sense for it to take a risk on.

Tip!

The key in a sales presentation is to deliver your pitch with confidence. If keeping all the numbers, pricing, and margins in your head makes you nervous, write them down. Better yet, write down your ideal distributor pricing plus several other acceptable possibilities that you can quickly glance at if you're questioned. If the distributor asks you if you can drop your distributor price or that they need to take a specific margin, you can quickly refer to your sheet and see what is workable without doing mental math in an already-stressful situation.

As you head into this meeting, have professional-looking, full-color sell sheets with you and be prepared to share your distributor pricing and other product details: net weight, case weight, and case dimensions. You might also be asked if you offer introductory pricing or programs or about other allowances you're willing to make, such as allowing free fills. (See chapter 18 for an explanation of common promotional terms.) Be sure that you've thought through your marketing strategy and are willing to convey what you are and are not willing to do.

THE FINE PRINT

If your sales meeting goes well and the distributor agrees to take you on, you will be asked to sign numerous forms. As always, before you sign any contracts or paperwork with a distributor, read it carefully and make sure you understand it.

Make sure that the contract or letter of agreement states how long it is good for and how either you or the distributor may terminate the relationship (how many days' notice is required, etc.). Because of the myriad ways that distributors seek to make money from their suppliers, you also need to fully comprehend the financial implications of the contract once all of the marketing allowances and other promotional costs are taken into account and make sure everything makes sense for your company. While as a small food producer you may not have tremendous leverage, you shouldn't be afraid to negotiate for your company's best interests. When in doubt, hire a business attorney to go over the contract too, and don't be afraid to walk away if the contract simply doesn't feel right for you.

Should I work with only one distributor?

An entrepreneur who was looking for distributors explained that he only wanted to work with one because he wanted to be loyal to them. While the decision of whether or not to work with multiple distributors is personal, you should remember that distributors are not technically loyal to you. Their loyalties lie with the retailers—they pay the distributors' bills. Distributors can and will drop your product if it doesn't meet their sales goals or isn't purchased by their retailers.

Also, because not every retailer works with every distributor, your relationships with distributors should not be exclusive. If you can keep up with the production demand, you should work with several distributors to increase your chances of getting into a number of stores. This distributor diversification also helps shelter you should stores you sell to change distributors. This does happen, and you would hate to have spent all that time and energy working with a distributor to get into your dream store only to have their contractual relationship end. If your target retailer decides to work with a different distributor, it can put you back at square one.

CHAPTER 11

SELLING TO THE SPECIALTY RETAIL CHANNEL

SPECIALTY RETAIL STORES RUN THE gamut from gourmet food stores to gift stores to coffee shops and small grocers that sell shelf-stable, packaged food products. These types of stores may focus specifically on a single ingredient or one region of the world. Or their businesses may center around unique food products that can't be found in typical supermarkets. Often, these retail stores are independently owned and have less than five locations.

Because these types of stores are smaller and may not have the sales volume of larger stores and supermarkets isn't reason to disregard them. Specialty retail stores actively seek out new products and brands that larger stores don't carry. This is how specialty retailers differentiate themselves from supermarkets. As such, these retailers are more willing to take a chance on new products and smaller producers like you.

They are also more likely to bring in products that are tied to the seasons or holidays, since that's another reason for customers to come into their stores time and time again. You could try pitching your products to them around those general themes. For example, your artisan salt may be the perfect complement to summer grilling seasons and/or make a great stocking stuffer for the holidays.

That being said, any new product the retailer brings in has to fit with the overall look and feel of that specialty store. Packaging is critical in these types of stores where customers may not be buying everyday items but something special for themselves, friends, or family.

Many times, the store buyer is also the store owner, so each has a significant personal and financial investment in making sure the products they sell are successful: that's what keeps customers coming back to them. Since these independent store buyers want reasons for their customers to shop them instead of a larger store, they may be more willing to bring your product in if you are willing to give them exclusivity within a certain town or area for a predefined amount of time. As the manufacturer, you may not want to offer exclusivity, but you should consider what can happen to your sales if you sell the products in question into larger stores: specialty retail buyers may no longer be interested in carrying your brand.

Specialty retail stores also typically have a more highly engaged and well-trained staff than your average supermarket. The staff takes pride in learning about the products the store carries, likes to highlight and explain product benefits to customers, and enjoys sharing the stories behind suppliers and products. The staff works to build relationships with customers and may even recommend a new product based on the customers' prior purchases.

GETTING INTO SPECIALTY RETAIL STORES

All of these factors work to your benefit, since the store will be actively engaged in selling your product and in helping to build a loyal brand following for your company. The fact that these types of retailers also prefer to work with relatively unknown brands makes them ideal for food companies that are just starting to sell wholesale. Unfortunately, getting in front of specialty food buyers is not always straightforward. Since the buyers tend to wear many hats—salesperson, store owner, human resources manager, bookkeeper, and so on, finding a time to pitch your product to them can be tough. Additionally, some specialty retail stores only work directly with food producers; others work solely with distributors or brokers, and others work with a combination of all of these.

Therefore, the best bet for your food business is to contact a store after you've done your due diligence and know that your product would fit in that location. Find out how their buyers prefer to see and evaluate new products. Unfortunately, this means a lot of cold calling and/or e-mailing to get clarity around their buying preferences. A recommendation from one specialty retail store buyer is to send along a postcard before you call. It should have a beautiful product image on one side and highlight your product's unique selling points on the other. Since the way a product looks is so important to specialty retail buyers, this can make a difference in how quickly your call or e-mail is returned.

Another option is to send product samples, but unsolicited samples can eat away at your budget fairly quickly. Many food entrepreneurs have had success via this route but only because they were committed to following up with the store buyer to set up a meeting.

MAINTAINING YOUR SHELF PRESENCE

Your job isn't done once your product hits the shelves at specialty food stores. Many artisan food entrepreneurs focus on opening as many new accounts as possible to increase revenue, but it is better to have fewer accounts that order regularly than many that only order once. Instead of focusing all your energy on opening that next new account, take a look at what you can do to increase sales within your existing accounts first.

Never forget that just because your product makes the initial cut and gets onto the shelf, that doesn't mean it's guaranteed to stay there. You need to work to ensure it stays on the shelf. You do this by building and cultivating a relationship with the store buyer and employees. Ask the retailer how often it wants you to drop by on sales calls. Offer to send product and company information to help train the staff or POP material for the store. Ask if you can come in and physically help restock product. Send relevant industry information that you think the store might find helpful. Ask about doing in-store demonstrations to help drive sales of your product. By the same token, don't be afraid to ask for feedback on your product. Stores see customers interact with your

> **Tip!**
>
> Make it easy for specialty retail store buyers to purchase from you by offering a smaller, "trial" order size that they can bring in to see if the product sells. Instead of a normal case of twelve units, for instance, offer a trial order of six units that includes at least one of each of your flavors so that the retailer gets a sense of how the products look merchandised together. This enables them to take a risk on bringing you in without a huge financial commitment.

products day in and day out, so they'll have a firm idea of what's working and what's not. Also, if you'll be offering a special promotion or if there's a change in your lead time at certain points in the year, let your buyers know so they can place orders in advance.

Spend the time to solidify your relationship with your existing buyers and ensure your product has good sales traction in a particular location before focusing too heavily on moving on to other new accounts. Slow, steady, and strategic will win this race and help prevent any future competitor from knocking you off the shelf.

The Benefits of In-Store Demonstrations

We've all seen demonstrations in stores from Costco to Whole Foods Market. The idea of standing in the aisle asking people to try your product may not be high on your list of ways you want to spend a Saturday afternoon, but in-store demos or sampling, if your product allows for it, should be high priority in your marketing plan if you're serious about getting into retail stores.

First, it's worth pointing out that not every store allows in-store demonstrations. Some, like Costco, have rules about who can and who can't perform them. Most specialty food stores welcome in-store demonstrations, but you should ask the buyer about it once he or she has expressed interest in your product. The benefit, both to you and to retailers, is that demonstrations typically increase product sales. New customers try something for the first time, and existing customers are reminded to purchase again.

In-store demonstrations cost you time and money (in product inventory), but there are other benefits beyond just increasing your sales within that store. They help you build your relationship with the buyer, signaling that you are committed to supporting your product and the store. (You can score extra brownie points by helping to drive traffic to that store—alert your friends and fans on social media about when and where your demo is). Being in the store for a few hours also gives you the opportunity to interact with employees and tell them the story behind your product and your company. This makes them more effective salespeople of your product when you're not there.

Just as important, though, in-store demonstrations allow you to build personal connections with consumers as well. This is your chance to get one-to-one with the customers, tell them your story, and turn them into supporters of your brand. As you talk to consumers, you also have a chance to get feedback about your product, your packaging, your price, and any other thoughts or ideas people have. Some of this may not be pleasant to hear, but even negative reactions to your product can help you fine-tune and craft your product and your messaging. Don't just listen to the feedback from people who try or buy your product but also solicit feedback from those who aren't interested and find out why. Are they loyal to a competitor's product? Do they simply not use food in this category? Do they have allergies they're concerned about? All of this feedback will help you craft a stronger message by learning more about who your target market is.

CHAPTER 12

SELLING TO MAIL-ORDER CATALOGS

THERE WAS A TIME NOT too long ago when the phrase "mail-order catalogs" meant the literal paper catalogs that stuff our mailboxes every holiday season. These days, though, almost every mail-order company has an online component that features hundreds of additional products that aren't listed in the print catalog. With more and more people too busy to go to physical stores, opening up wholesale accounts with mail-order companies can be a huge boost to your bottom line and, depending on the companies you work with, can further build your brand awareness as well.

UNDERSTANDING HOW MAIL-ORDER COMPANIES WORK

Mail order companies work a little differently than traditional brick-and-mortar stores in that they have two options when offering products to their customers. They may ask about purchasing inventory from you, similar to any brick-and-mortar store. This is inventory that they pay for, hold in their warehouses, and deliver to customers as orders come in. The second way mail order catalogs work is via drop-shipping.

For food products especially, drop-shipping is fairly common among catalog and Internet retailers. Certain products are offered for sale, but the retailers don't actually carry inventory of them. Instead, the retailer passes the order along to you, the producer, and you fill and ship the order. You then charge the retailer your drop-ship price (your wholesale price plus a little bit extra to cover the shipping box and handling costs), and the retailer makes money on the margin between the drop-ship price and the retail price they charge the consumer.

As an example, Hot Mama's Salsa company is approached by a mail-order company buyer about being a drop-ship partner. The retailer puts pictures and descriptions of Hot Mama's Salsa on its website and in its catalog. Customer Susan in New Hampshire gets her catalog and thinks Hot Mama's Salsa would be the perfect gift for her sister, so she places an order. Susan is charged $32.99, which includes all shipping and taxes.

The catalog company sends the recorded order to Hot Mama's Salsa. Most larger online and catalog companies work through automated drop-ship software that e-mails orders, shipping information, and prepaid packing labels directly to their drop-ship vendors. Hot Mama's boxes up the order and sends it on its way to New Hampshire.

After the order has shipped, Hot Mama's invoices the mail-order company for the drop-ship price of $12.00. Again, with larger mail order companies, this can all take place within the drop-ship software. Then the mail-order company pays the invoice based on the agreed-upon net terms.

PROS OF DROP-SHIPPING

By partnering with another company—especially a larger, more established company—you open your products and your brand to a wider audience. Strategic partnerships can also help elevate your own brand. For example, if you partner with a company like Williams-Sonoma or Neiman Marcus, it helps reassure customers that your products meet a high level of quality as opposed to if customers had found your randomly online on their own. All of this combined means the potential for increased revenue.

CONS OF DROP-SHIPPING

There can be drawbacks to drop-shipping. You have to make sure you have enough inventory or can make enough product fast enough to fill orders that may come in at any time. The risk here, of course, is that if you do have a lot of inventory and the sales don't happen, then you carry the inventory cost, not the catalog company.

You also need to have shipping boxes, packing material, and the staff available so that you can fulfill orders quickly. To get the best rates on packaging, you may have to buy hundreds of boxes of specific shapes. This is a cost you have to pay for up front, and you won't recoup it until all those boxes have been used for orders.

As a drop-ship partner, you have to pack orders in line with the mail-order company's specifications. For instance, some will let you pack a complete order into one box whereas other companies want each item packed and shipped in its own, separate box. You also can't add any marketing material or other means to try to turn these customers into your own, direct customers.

You will typically be on net terms with these retailers. Even if you ship the box out today, you may not be paid for thirty, forty-five, or even sixty days. Again that is a cost to you, because that is cash you don't have access to.

THINGS TO CONSIDER BEFORE SIGNING DROP-SHIPPING AGREEMENTS:

Does the company you're talking to have the cachet to be worthy of drop-shipping? It may make sense to agree to drop-ship for a big name like Dean & Deluca, where you know your product will be exposed to hundreds of thousands of people, but the time, energy, and cost that goes into drop-shipping may not make sense for you for new internet companies that have limited customer databases. Don't underestimate the stress involved in keeping a substantial drop-ship inventory ready to go for drop-ship orders—especially around the holidays! You should align yourself only with strong drop-ship partners who will help enhance your business.

You need to make sure you understand how the drop-ship partner will communicate orders to you? The seamless automated systems that larger companies use, once you're familiar with them, are fairly straightforward. I've talked to other, smaller mail order retailers, though, who use different means for getting orders out—some of which are seamless and some of which seem to entail jumping through four hoops and doing a jig before the order is processed. Make sure that whatever process you're considering makes sense for your business and won't add significantly to your workload.

To save on costs, you should see if you can find one or two shipping box sizes that will work for all your packaging needs so you don't have to purchase twenty different box sizes. Maybe all you need is a small package for just a single product and a medium or large box for orders you receive for multiple products.

Since you have to pay for the boxes and the packing material (not to mention the time to pack up individual orders), be sure to reflect these costs in the wholesale price you present to drop-ship partners.

These items (and time!) are costs above and beyond your typical wholesale price, so make sure you're reimbursed for them.

Without doubt, all products should be shipped on the mail-order company's account number. You should not pay up front to ship. No matter how big or small the drop-ship partner is, if it is not willing to provide you with a shipping account number, seriously consider walking away. A catalog or online store that does a lot of shipping can command a better shipping rate than you can. From your standpoint, as well, if you're not being paid on the order for thirty to sixty days anyway, you don't want to float an additional $15 or $30 more in shipping charges that you're waiting to be reimbursed for. That's money you can use today to help grow your business. It may not sound like much now, but when you have a hundred orders you're waiting to be paid on and $15 in shipping added to each one, then that's a lot of money tied up that you can't use elsewhere!

> These days, as you well know, thousands of online stores mail items to their customers. Even though stand-alone Internet stores often don't have physical catalogs or brick-and-mortar stores, they often operate like catalog companies, so you can follow the same recommendations when working with them.

FINDING AND WORKING WITH MAIL-ORDER CATALOG BUYERS

You may need to do some sleuthing to find buyers for mail-order companies, but it's certainly not impossible. Start by asking your network of friends, family, and contacts to see if anyone as a connection to someone at a company you're interested in approaching. Some food brokers also have contacts into mail order companies and may be able to help get your products in.

Barring any direct connections to mail-order company buyers, you can search company websites for information on how to submit new products for consideration. A handful of companies offer this information publicly. Alternatively, you could call companies to get instructions or ask who you should talk with about submitting products.

The most successful avenue for finding mail-order company buyers, though, is to let them find you—at trade shows. The major companies send buyers to the big food-industry trade shows every year to look for new products, so this might be your opportunity. You shouldn't pigeonhole yourself into food-specific shows, though. Depending on the type of mail-order company and the variety of products it carries, buyers also attend gift shows and sometimes even regional shows. Unfortunately, trade shows can be a bit of a gamble, as they can be significantly expensive to attend, and there's no guarantee that a catalog buyer will approach you.

> LinkedIn is a great tool to see if someone you're connected to can make an introduction to a key buyer for you. This not only works well to connect with mail-order buyers but other buyers as well.

Because of how mail order typically works, if you exhibit at a trade show, you should determine in advance if you're open to drop-ship arrangements. If so, be prepared with your drop-ship price and decide which of your products are available for drop-shipping. (See chapter 17 for more about exhibiting at trade shows.)

Just like every retailer you work with, mail-order buyers deserve attention after you've successfully opened an account. Follow up with them after the first few months and see if they're willing to provide feedback on how your products are performing compared to other, similar products. These buyers may also have recommendations or new product ideas for you based on what they see selling successfully through their channels.

> **Timing Is Key When Approaching Mail-Order Company Buyers**
>
> Typically, catalog company buyers work eight to ten months in advance. This is because it takes this much time to have a catalog shot, created, produced, and printed. So, while you're focused on Valentine's Day, they're already planning what they'll offer in December. A mail-order buyer can't do anything with your holiday product in October; it's too late for them to add. If you want to get into mail-order catalogs, you need to be as forward-thinking as the buyers and pitch your products to them in a timely manner.

CHAPTER 13

SELLING TO SUPERMARKETS

SUPERMARKETS COME IN MANY SHAPES and forms these days. Experts technically call this channel "food, drug, mass"—it encompasses everything from traditional supermarkets to drugstores to mass retailers like Target and Walmart. Of course, we'll focus on the food portion here.

Within the food category of supermarkets, there are actually three separate subcategories: gourmet, natural, and traditional grocery. "Gourmet" retailers are stores like D'Agostino and Zabar's; "natural" grocers are stores like Whole Foods Market and New Seasons, and "traditional" grocers are stores like Albertsons and Safeway. Each of these subcategories is broken into national and regional players.

Typically, no matter what type of food supermarket these stores are, they average around twenty thousand square feet or more (though new smaller square footage formats are being played with in certain markets in recent years) with most of their space devoted to food and food products. With thousands of products of all types, supermarkets are obviously major shopping destinations. Most nonrestaurant food dollars in North America are spent in supermarkets.

Because supermarkets draw a large clientele, food entrepreneurs are often focused on getting their products into those stores. This makes sense, given that supermarkets provide customers with an easily accessible and reliable place to buy their products and serve such a large number of customers every week. Additionally, these types of stores typically carry far more food products than stand-along specialty retailers. Considering that these types of stores may have tens, hundreds, or even thousands of locations, you can see how sales could quickly add up.

This isn't to say that there aren't complications in selling to supermarkets. Beyond the basic act of getting your product onto shelves, you face an uphill battle in getting customers to actually purchase your products. Think of your average trip to the supermarket. How much time do you spend scouring the aisles in search of products that are new to you? When and if you find those products, how often do you purchase them having never tried them before?

This is why developing a marketing plan for supermarkets is so critical. Big food brands spend millions of dollars to advertise their products to consumers because consumer recognition equals increased sales. While you may not have nearly the marketing budget to spend that the big brands do, it is naive to think that your product can be successful on supermarket shelves without some type of marketing support behind it. Chapter 16 has more information about promotions that you can integrate into your supermarket marketing plan.

FINDING SUPERMARKET BUYERS

Due to sheer volume of products that supermarkets carry, they typically have numerous buyers who each overseas different product categories (they are also sometimes referred to as category managers). How these buyers make decisions varies from store to store. In some stores, the buying decisions are made at the store level while other supermarkets have their buyers centralized at corporate headquarters and make the purchasing decisions for the entire chain. To add a little more complexity, some stores are willing to review new products at any time while others have specific times during the year, normally called "category reviews," when they review the performance of all products within a specific category to decide which will go and which new products to bring on.

As you can guess, finding the right supermarket buyer is not without its challenges. First, you must identify whether the store makes decisions on a regional or national level, then identify the correct buyer who manages the category your product falls into, and then approach them during the right time of year. This is where a good food broker can be especially helpful. Brokers who have relationships with national or regional supermarkets can help guide you through the supermarkets' buying process and make the right introductions for you. A good food broker can also help you determine the right marketing strategy for keeping your product in a store based on the specifics of its marketplace.

To successfully get onto supermarket shelves, you may also need to work with a distributor who takes care of the logistics of getting your product to the stores. As mentioned in the "Working with Distributors" chapter, supermarkets want to limit how many people drop product off at their stores, so most choose to work through distributors.

> If you're interested in getting your products onto supermarket shelves, consider starting with regional supermarket chains. Those buyers may be more willing to consider your product since you're a "local" producer.

WHAT SUPERMARKET BUYERS ARE LOOKING FOR

Make no mistake: supermarket buyers want to offer customers the best mix of products, but they are also highly analytical and focused on the metrics of every single product within their category. Their job performance is typically measured on how quickly their category's products sell as well as the profit margin it generates for the company. For your product to get onto their shelves, you must be prepared to make a strong analytical case for why your product is a good fit for their company. And to stay on their shelves, your product must prove itself in performance. This is why having a strong marketing plan is so critical.

If you can arrange a meeting with a regional or national supermarket buyer, come prepared to the meeting with not only your wholesale price points but also any sales history you can share with the buyer to prove that your product needs to be on their shelves. Include information about your best-selling products, anything you've learned about your target consumer to date, or data points from other stores, such as how often their inventory of your product sells out and they reorder.

> Keep in mind that as you move into supermarkets, you may lose independent specialty store accounts. This is because those stores want to offer products that are not found at supermarkets. Therefore, you need to weigh the impact a potential loss of accounts will have on your business against the potential upside that increased distribution through supermarkets may bring you.

You need to build a strong case for why you deserve to be on their shelves while also showcasing what you plan to do from a marketing standpoint to get their customers to purchase your products. Chapter 16 has more information about different types of promotional support you may want to consider, but in addition to that, you should also speak to how you'll support your product via online and/or traditional advertising campaigns. Also ask about the opportunity to do in-store demonstrations. While not every store allows for them—and they take a lot of time and energy to do—this can be one of the quickest ways to build brand awareness among a store's customers. It can help you grow your sales quickly and show the buyer that your product deserves its shelf space.

CHAPTER 14

SELLING TO DRUG, MASS, AND CLUB STORES

SELLING TO DRUG AND MASS STORES

We've noted that the supermarket channel is broken into three main segments—food, drug, and mass. We won't go into depth on the drug and mass channels because they're not where most food entrepreneurs at this stage are interested in putting their time and energy. It's good to know a little about these channels, though, in case you ever decide to consider them.

You can guess that getting your product onto Target store shelves across the country or into every Walgreens could be a huge boon to your bottom line. The sheer quantity of product that these types of stores can move can make your brand a household name. All of this, though, comes with a price.

To get your products onto the shelves of stores like these, you may have to be prepared to spend thousands of dollars on production—possibly millions—to meet demand. There is also the additional marketing spend required by these stores, as they want to know that you're going to support your products with advertising and promotional campaigns. You may notice that most of the brands currently on these shelves are big brands to begin with. That's because they have production capability and advertising support. Most people reading this book at this juncture are not in this league. That isn't to say that down the road, after your business has grown or has found outside sources of capital through private equity investment or a line of credit, this might not be a viable option for you. Before you make that move, though, you must be financially prepared to do so.

Not every product or brand fits into drug and/or mass stores. These types of stores focus on providing their customers with good value for their money and often use low prices to attract them. If your specialty food product has a higher price point or the brand you're developing is focused on the high-end, luxury consumer, then these types of stores are not a good fit for your overall business strategy.

You may be able to grow into these big box retailers. Give your business and your brand recognition time to grow, and one day you may get there. It's happened to more than one food manufacturer who started out with nothing more than a dream and an idea. Along the way, though, these businesses picked up key employees, advisors, and the financial means to make it happen.

SELLING TO CLUB STORES

Selling to club stores like Sam's and Costco offers many of the same benefits as selling into the drug and mass stores: your product becomes very widely available. But this audience approaches a shopping experience as a "treasure hunt." Because the product mix in these stores changes constantly, not only are customers looking for what is new and different, but buyers are more open to new products because of the limited time they'll spend on the shelf.

This isn't to suggest that club stores are open to products that haven't been tested in the marketplace. A product that is new to the club store still needs a proven sales history behind it to be considered. Though the inventory the club's buyers bring in is only there for a limited time, that doesn't make its real estate any less valuable. Like supermarket, drug, and mass buyers, club buyers are measured on their sales figures, so they are focused on making smart, strategic buying decisions.

One way in which club stores shine that benefits smaller food companies is that club buyers are more often willing than drug and mass buyers to consider products that have had strong regional success but don't yet have national distribution. Club buyers also have the latitude to determine whether to bring products in on a local store level, which is ideal for new product trials, or regionally or nationally. Products in club stores may also need less advertising support because of their consumers' mind-set: the shopping experience is their opportunity to find new and interesting items. This isn't to suggest, however, that no promotional support at all is required. If you've ever spent any time in club stores, you know that food product demonstrations are quite popular, and you, the manufacturer, will be required to provide a demo budget.

Like drug and mass stores, before you consider trying to enter club stores, there are a few things you need to consider. Are club stores the right location for your products and your brand? Equally as important, how might club store distribution impact your other sales channel accounts? Specialty stores certainly don't want to find that their customers can buy the products they carry in bulk at the club store. Even stores like Whole Foods Market are starting to pull back on products that opt into club stores.

You know you must have the funds necessary to meet the production demands a club store may require, but you also need money to develop and provide packaging that meets the club's needs. Since club stores tend to specialize in bulk selling, you might have to develop new packaging altogether or determine how your products can be shrink-wrapped together. Last, due to club stores' desire to offer their customers the best possible price points, a club buyer may try to negotiate a significant discount with you due to the volume of product the store is willing to purchase. As always, ensure that any agreement on final price provides enough profit margin for you to continue to grow your business.

FINDING DRUG, MASS, AND CLUB BUYERS

While drug, mass, and club buyers all attend the major industry trade shows and may even approach you if your company has a booth, to successfully sell into these channels it is best to have expert advice and guidance. There are food brokers who specialize in these channels and who can make the right introductions for you. They can also guide you through the pitch process and negotiations and provide feedback that can help your business thrive in these channels.

CHAPTER 15

SELLING TO FOOD SERVICE AND HOSPITALITY

THERE'S AN INCREASED DEMAND BY today's consumers, restauranteurs, and chefs to use local, artisan-produced specialty food products as ingredients in or complements to restaurant meals. This offers specialty food entrepreneurs another channel through which to sell products and help build brand recognition.

All food service operations are not created equal, though. A large institution such as a government-funded nursing home, which is undoubtedly a food service organization, may not necessarily be interested in your handcrafted products. These types of larger accounts are usually served via distributors and are much more focused on lowering their costs as much as possible. This cost focus makes it hard for small food businesses to successfully compete because food entrepreneurs have a harder time competing with large manufacturers on price.

This doesn't mean that food service isn't a category you shouldn't go after. If it makes sense for your product, you might find a niche in selling to restaurants, food trucks, or other food providers. Similarly, hotels may be willing to carry your products as thank-you gifts for guests. Depending on your brand and your goals, having an account with a hospitality company like the Four Seasons may help solidify for retailers that your products are worth carrying.

Similarly, these days more and more corporations are offering their employees occasional perks, like free food from local food providers. Also, if you live in a port town, don't forget about the immense purchasing power of cruise ships. They may want to provide an artisan-made treat to their guests.

Toffee Talk, a small, San Francisco-based toffee company, sells hundreds of packages of their toffee to Google's corporate offices every week—which employees get to devour during their late-night coding sessions. How'd they pull it off? Toffee Talk's Ellin Purdom happened to meet a woman at a bus stop whose sister was a Google employee, so Ellin shared a business card and a sample of toffee with her. And the rest, as they say, is history.

OPENING FOOD SERVICE AND HOSPITALITY ACCOUNTS

Use the same approach to opening food service and hospitality accounts as you take with independent specialty stores. While some food brokers have relationships that can help you get into places like this, most of the time, it's up to you to cold call and send samples to get your foot in the door. Networking can also be hugely beneficial in this realm, as chefs talk to other chefs, concierges talk to other hotel concierges, and so on. Do what you can to maximize the connections you have and look for opportunities to make more in areas where you might be lacking.

Convenience Stores and Gas Stations

In recent years, convenience stores and gas stations have begun to focus more energy on their food product offerings. This is due in part to the fact that their historical offerings of gasoline, alcohol, and tobacco are so highly regulated there is limited profitability in those items for stores. These stores have also recognized that consumers are more and more seeking 'grab and go' snacks and meals. This m akes the convenience and gas station market one of the fastest growing segments for food sales. Between the snack food on their shelves to new, expanded prepared food options that go far beyond roller grill items, for the right type of products, these stores could prove to be highly profitable.

CHAPTER 16

SUPPORTING YOUR RETAILERS

WE'VE EMPHASIZED THAT GETTING ONTO the shelf is one thing, while staying there is another thing entirely. After all the time and effort of opening a new account, your work has only just begun. A retailer has given you and your company a chance by giving up some of their coveted shelf space to bring your product(s) on, and you should be willing to do everything possible to support that retailer and help drive more customers to their stores. Not only does this demonstrate that you view the store as a partner and not simply a channel through which to sell your product, you'll also increase your own sales. So really, it's a win-win!

Laying the Foundation of a Good Retailer Relationship

KEEP YOUR RETAIL PRICE POINTS CONSISTENT

The number-one thing in maintaining a good relationship with your retailers is not to offer your products directly to customers at less than your MSRP. While you can't control what retailers actually charge for your products, you shouldn't undercut them yourself. This doesn't mean you can't put items on sale from time to time, but do so in a limited manner and only when it makes strategic sense.

HELP PEOPLE FIND THEIR STORES

Take advantage of tools that can help drive sales to your retail stores: on your website, include a list of (and/or links to) the retailers who carry your products. Similarly, call out your retailers in your social media or e-newsletter from time to time to let customers know they can find your products in their favorite stores as well.

FOLLOW UP WITH STORE BUYERS

Buyers are, without a doubt, incredibly busy. But few will think poorly of you if you call after they've placed an order to see how the products are selling. This is also a great opportunity to ask whether the buyer has recommendations on specific point-of-purchase material or staff training information the store might need, or even if you can do an in-store demonstration. By showing the retailer that you are doing everything possible to develop a long-term relationship, it will be more willing to do everything it can to help your product succeed.

PROMOTIONS: TERMS AND PHRASES

Retailers want the best deal possible for themselves and their customers. You may be asked about one or more types of promotions. Rather than say yes immediately, only to run to the Internet afterwards to find out what you've just agreed to, here are some of the most common terms and phrases you'll hear regarding promotions.

A **MANUFACTURER'S COUPON** is a discount offer for retail customers. Coupons are delivered in several ways, including via direct mail, e-mail, on manufacturer social media sites, on product packages, or through mobile devices. It's well known that discounts encourage sales.

The manufacturer covers the cost of this promotion, so you must consider how stores would redeem coupons back to you and collect the money they're owed. While larger companies use clearinghouses to facilitate these transactions, most small businesses can't afford clearinghouses and choose self-redemption instead. Someone must oversee the redemption process, and you need a clear plan for it that retailers can easily understand and follow.

An **IN-AD COUPON** (or *retailer coupon*) is similar to the above, but it is delivered to customers via retailers' own marketing material (such as mailed circulars). Your retailers may have e-newsletters or social media sites or run print ads in magazines and newspapers where you could offer their customers discounts directly. This also shows the retailer that you are committed to looking after their customers. Again, you'll need to work out how the store recovers the cost of the promotion after the fact.

An **INSTANT REDEEMABLE COUPON** is another type of manufacturer's coupon that can be used immediately upon checkout. In most cases, it's affixed directly to packaging to help convince customers to try a product when they see it in the aisle. For small specialty food businesses, though, the cost of creating and implementing these is an added hurdle along with the existing issue of ensuring the store recovers its costs.

AD SUPPORT (OR ADVERTISING ALLOWANCE) is an agreed-upon amount (either fixed or as a percentage of sales) that a manufacturer pays a retailer to advertise within the retailer's usual channels. This might include paying a store to mention a brand in its newspaper ads or circulars. This method is less often seen at the independent specialty store level, but it is certainly common when you work with larger stores and distributors.

We've already discussed **IN-STORE DEMONSTRATIONS. IN-STORE SAMPLING** also allows the customer to try before they buy, but this version is often done by a store employee (as at Costco, for example) rather than the food artisan.

A **SAMPLING ALLOWANCE** enables retailers to give out samples to customers. It is typically offered through a lower price per case on the total order, or it is done as a percentage of the total order that is credited back to the retailer.

FREE GOODS (sometimes also called *free fill*) is similar to a sampling allowance. The retailer can sample product without incurring costs. Sampling allowances are done through a cash exchange, though, whereas free goods or free fill are where the manufacturer sends a specific number of free units that can be used for sampling along with the order.

> Sampling can be a huge driver of sales for both you and your retailers, especially if you have a product that people aren't familiar with. However, you must price your products right in the first place so that you have the wiggle room to cover promotions like this.

A **TEMPORARY PRICE REDUCTION** is one of the easiest promotions for small food companies to enact. You lower your product's price temporarily and stipulate that the savings be passed on to the customer. Most retailers require a promotional fee to run reductions like this. A food entrepreneur should be reasonably sure that a temporary price reduction, which nets a lower profit, will translate into enough customer purchases to offset the profit loss and cover the promotional fee.

We've noted that **POP MATERIAL** is point-of-purchase material that is typically printed. But there is a move toward creating POP videos and other more interactive media for communicating a food business's message to consumers within stores. POP might include shelf signs, small posters, or even add-ons to your packaging—like a small card on a ribbon that complements the package and tells the consumer even more of your story. POP material is not meant for offering discounts but to catch consumers' attention and pique enough interest in your product for them to take it home and try it.

The POP landscape is changing these days. Some stores permit—or even specifically ask for—manufacturer POP material to help them engage with customers, whereas others require all POP material to be produced by their own creative team for a consistent look throughout the store. Some stores, though, are moving away from all POP material for a streamlined, cleaner, less-cluttered look. Ask buyers what they prefer.

A **BOGO** is an in-store promotion that means "buy one, get one [free]." Sometimes this is changed slightly to "buy one, get the second half-off." In this type of promotion, the manufacturer almost always covers the cost of the additional product.

If your product requires special handling (perhaps it must be kept frozen) or if your coupon redemption program requires the store to do extra steps, you may be asked to pay a *handling allowance* to cover the cost associated with the additional work.

Yes, **SLOTTING FEES**, the most feared of promotions, do actually exist. Thankfully, slotting fees are typically only used by larger stores (and in some cases, distributors), and you may run into them as you grow your wholesale business. Specifically, slotting fees are paid by the manufacturer to secure space—a "slot"—on the shelf.

As we've mentioned, when you get on a shelf, it usually means someone else is coming off. Some retailers try to negotiate a *buy-out allowance* in which you pay a fee to remove a competitor's goods from the shelves in order for yours to go on. Usually, this is tied to the retail value of the goods that your products replace.

OFF-INVOICE DEDUCTIONS are fairly common among distributors, but they're certainly used by retailers as well. They are agreed-upon temporary price reductions on your product that are automatically applied to the retailer's or distributor's invoice. For example, if you sell three cases of product to a retailer for $3.99 but have an agreement for an off-invoice deduction of 10 percent per case, then you only bill them for $3.59 per case.

KNOWING WHEN PROMOTIONS MAKE SENSE FOR YOU

The above list is certainly not exhaustive, but as you can see, there are numerous ways you can work with retailers to incentivize customers to purchase your product. Of course, such promotions do cost you money, either in the form of cash or free product, so it's critical that you evaluate each promotion carefully and be sure that it makes sense for you. While you want to develop good relationships with your buyers (and distributors), you shouldn't feel forced into promotions that don't help you meet your objectives.

By the same token, don't be afraid to negotiate the terms of promotions. Nothing is written in stone until the agreement is signed, so try to strike the best possible bargain for yourself while keeping the retailer's needs and goals in mind. Also, don't be afraid to think outside the box. Based on what you know about your retailers, you could very well come up with a promotion that is not listed here. If you think it will work and makes sense for both you and the retailer, ask about it. Stores, like everyone else, are open to new ideas that help drive traffic and sales.

Sometimes it's impossible to know in advance whether a promotion will have its intended impact, but before you embark on any promotion, make sure you understand all of its costs to you. Weigh whether your other retailers will see the promotion and request the same deal. Could you afford to do it? After a promotion has ended, evaluate its success based on accurate sales figures and

> It is helpful to develop a marketing plan for your wholesale business that includes a promotional schedule. This allows you to plan out, in advance, when you're going to offer promotions to retailers, what those promotions will look like, and how those promotions tie into your other marketing efforts. By creating this promotional schedule (ideally looking forward for several months or even a year), you can make sure your promotions are inline with your business goals and make good financial sense while also enabling you to be prepared from a product inventory standpoint.

costs and determine whether you made or lost money. If you profited, use the promotion again in the future, but if you took a loss, don't reuse it unless you can rework it in a way that makes financial sense.

CHAPTER 17

GROWING YOUR WHOLESALE BUSINESS VIA TRADE SHOWS

TRADE SHOWS PROVIDE THE OPPORTUNITY to showcase your company and your products to a large audience of buyers, brokers, sales representatives, and distributors all in a single setting. Usually taking place over multiple days, trade shows enable you to build in-person relationships and to address questions or concerns face-to-face.

Before we continue, let's make a distinction between trade shows and festivals or other events where large groups of people gather. Trade shows are typically not open to the general public. They are business-to-business events with the express purpose of creating wholesale relationships. Trade shows are not events at which you sell goods directly to the public. There are some hybrid models, which limit participants to qualified buyers for a specified period and then open the doors to the public. In these instances, approach the first part like a trade show and the second part like a consumer show.

Some small businesses, in an effort to make every event they attend as profitable as possible, question time spent at trade shows versus retail-focused consumer events where they can sell their product directly to the public. Whereas retail-focused consumer shows provide you with the short-term benefit of sales today, trade shows should be approached with a long term outlook. While you may not be able to physically sell inventory today at a trade show, what you're hoping to do there is build relationships with buyers who will help you grow your wholesale business via repeat purchase orders.

OTHER BENEFITS OF TRADE SHOWS

- Many trade shows have areas specifically for first-time exhibitors. They give buyers a quick way to find out who or what is new.

✎ Getting in front of hundreds or even thousands of buyers at one event can help to drive down your marketing costs. This breadth of exposure can also cut down on the time you spend attempting to open individual accounts.

✎ You can write a lot of orders at a trade show. Don't think you'll walk out of a trade show without any sales. Buyers there actively seek new and interesting products and companies, many intending to spend money and write orders.

✎ Of course, not everyone you meet at trade shows will order, but that doesn't mean that those relationships lack value. Capture information from every buyer you meet to build your sales database. Though one buyer may not be a customer today, he or she could be a customer tomorrow as long as you maintain contact.

✎ Entrepreneurship can be lonely at times. Trade shows provide a great venue to meet with other entrepreneurs. Develop these relationships, and you'll have allies who can help you through your struggles. They may even help you dislodge some of the big brands from store shelves to make room for your products.

✎ You can conduct research by walking a trade show floor. It's a great way to gather information about your competitors and to keep an eye on which way the industry as a whole is trending. As an aside, I don't advocate approaching competitors for information by pretending to be a buyer. If you do approach a competitor at a trade show, identify yourself and your company up front so that your competitor can decide what information they do or don't want to share. If you're not comfortable doing that, simply walking near the booth of a competitor can give you a wealth of information about their products, their packaging, and even how they're positioning their company with respect to buyers.

FINDING THE RIGHT TRADE SHOWS FOR YOUR COMPANY

No matter what type of product your company makes, a trade show exists for you. Plug your product type and the phrase "trade show" into any search engine, and chances are, you'll receive more results than you know what to do with. In addition to the many large, national food trade shows that take place during the year, there are countless smaller, regional shows throughout the country. Gift shows or holiday-themed trade shows can also provide small food businesses with a great return on investment. Many of their buyers look for specialty gifts or seasonal products to offer customers.

With so many trade shows to choose from, how do you decide which one is right for you? Consider the following:

Are your buyers there? Based on what you know about your target retail audience, would your buyers attend this show? If you're focused on local specialty store buyers, you may find more success in attending a local trade show over a national one.

What are the numbers? Ask for data. The glossy trade show brochures proclaim that thousands of buyers flock through their doors. Be sure that the numbers you're looking at reflect net attendance versus gross attendance. Gross attendance counts *every* person who walks in, while net attendance excludes exhibitors, press, those with complimentary passes to the show, and so forth. If such information isn't readily available, don't be afraid to ask show management for specifics before you sign up for a booth. Similarly, look at other information, like attendee demographics, to determine if the buyers

Take trade show attendee data that you receive with a grain of salt. Trade show associations often count every single person who walks through the door to inflate numbers and make their shows more attractive to exhibitors. Ask for a breakdown of buyers, distributors, brokers, sales representatives, and press. Ask for the exact number of organizations that attended the previous show. If one store sends three buyers to a show, trade show attendee data usually counts them as three separate individuals even though they represent only one company and one buying decision. Also, ask if trade show attendees are qualified buyers. In other words, are the buyers required to show some type of proof that they're affiliated with the industry prior to being allowed to participate? This helps to keep the general public out of these events, allowing you to maximize your time talking to potential buyers.

attending will be from the type of store that you hope to attract and from a geographic region that's a good fit for your product. Your hot cocoa may be delicious, but at a trade show made up of mostly buyers from Florida, you may have a hard time getting the interest you'd like. *What are my goals at trade shows?* Going to trade shows simply to attend can quickly become expensive. Knowing in advance what you hope to achieve will help you determine which trade shows are right for you and your products. Having goals also help you stay focused at the show itself. Goals should be specific and measurable: how many connections made, leads generated, or orders placed.

Which shows make the most sense? Many small businesses figure they should throw all their eggs into the biggest basket, hoping to get into the largest national trade shows and in front of the most buyers. Though that approach may be sound, if you're not distributed nationally or don't have the capability to quickly ramp up production, smaller or regional shows may make more sense. The big national shows will always be there. First, go to the show that makes the most sense for where you and your business stand today. This helps you grow your business in a smart manner, steadily working toward the next level.

How much will the show cost? For small businesses, expenses are always of paramount concern. You want to be sure that every dollar you spend is spent wisely. Carefully calculate how much a show will cost you. The most obvious expense is the exhibition or booth space. Do you also first have to join a specific association and pay dues? Further, factor in your travel and lodging costs. How much it will cost to get your booth set up at the event? Will you need to ship your booth exhibit and sample products to the site? These expenses can add up quickly and may limit which trade shows you can attend.

Tip!

Cut your exhibiting costs by partnering with other small businesses. If you're shipping items to a show, you may be able to share a pallet with another business from your area. Sharing hotel rooms or rental cars can help save money, too.

What do others recommend? Ask other small businesses for feedback about shows they've attended. Once again, this is where building relationships with other entrepreneurs can come in handy.

BEFORE THE TRADE SHOW

Once you've figured out which trade show(s) to attend, your work has just begun. Since you've committed your time and money, do everything in your power to achieve the goals you've set.

DESIGNING YOUR TRADE SHOW BOOTH

A trade show booth is a set amount of space on the trade show floor. That's pretty much what you're paying for. It's up to you to turn that blank slate into something appealing, something that will stand out and catch the attention of buyers as they walk through the aisles. Keep in mind that with so many other businesses and booths in a single area, your booth needs to break through the clutter, quickly and effectively telling the story of your company and your product.

Put yourself in the buyer's shoes for a minute. Imagine yourself at an enormous convention center with over two thousand exhibitors in attendance. Each exhibitor is vying for your attention and you have just a limited amount of time to see what's there before you get back on the road. You're tired, your feet hurt, and you're getting a little frustrated with being jostled by the crowd. You quickly walk up and down the corridors, smartphone in hand, simultaneously checking e-mails as you take it all in.

As food business owner and booth exhibitor, you have mere seconds to catch the buyer's attention. That's why you must design a booth that's pleasing to look at and clearly conveys what your company does without any verbal input from you. The truth of the matter is that no matter how friendly you are, you simply won't have the chance to talk to every buyer. Your booth design must do the majority of the work for you.

To create the most successful boot display, start by visualizing the space you'll be renting. Better yet, mark out an equivalent space in your house, yard, or office/kitchen. Once you have the space marked, ask yourself how you can use it to clearly show buyers what your product does and why they should stop to talk to you. You might use photography (especially enlarged images of your product that can be seen well from five to seven feet away), samples, pop-up screens, and signage to help you tell your company story and to entice people to visit your booth to learn more.

As you begin to consider furniture, keep in mind that you want a space that allows for flow. Trade show corridors can be very busy. You want to give buyers the opportunity to step into your booth and out of the commotion as they learn a bit more about your products. Entering your booth should feel both inviting and relaxing to buyers. You don't want them to feel like they must stay in the corridor, being brushed by passersby, to have a simple conversation.

Some trade show organizations or venues rent out furniture at an added cost. While smaller shows may have limited options, larger shows often provide a wider range, including podiums, couches, and even carpeting to make your booth look more welcoming. Renting furniture may cost you extra, but it does make your booth feel more welcoming, and you don't have to marshal it yourself. It will be placed in your booth space for you, and after the show, you leave the pieces there for someone else to pick up. Renting can be a great option for anyone who doesn't want to struggle with large, unwieldy pieces or who can't or doesn't want to bring their own. If you're just getting started and want to be sure that your booth looks professional before making any real capital investments, renting furniture can be worth it.

On the flip side, thanks to companies like IKEA, The Home Depot, The Container Store, and others, it is possible to furnish a booth without breaking the bank. If you do shop for trade show furniture, look for pieces that allow more flexible booth design so you can reuse them year after year. Note that many trade shows prohibit the use of power tools, unless you hire their union laborers at additional cost, so look for easy assembly and disassembly of furniture by hand or with a simple socket wrench. Light furniture will serve you best when carrying or shipping it. You may even combine purchased furniture and rentals from the trade show organization. Pieces that really complement your booth design may be worth purchasing; you can always rent additional pieces as needed.

BOOTH DESIGN TIPS

- Any product photography in your booth should be of professional quality. This may be one of your main forms of marketing material. Simply blowing up a picture that you took with your smartphone in so-so lighting will reflect poorly on your product.

- If your product is small, make sure to show it at eye level. Strategically place graphics or sample packaging throughout your booth.

- Lighting at trade shows is notoriously poor. Often, the large, overhead lights glare down, creating strange shadows or washing out your product. If you can afford it, consider paying to have electricity pulled to your booth and bring additional lighting. The Home Depot, Lowe's, and other home improvement stores sell cheap lights with metal clamps that are nearly weightless. They can easily be clamped onto any part of your booth where the lighting appears lower than you'd prefer.

- If your company or products have won any awards, consider incorporating them into your booth design. Use the physical award itself or mention it in some of your signage. This shows buyers that your product has already been validated and that they should check it out.

- Make your booth look as if it is full of product—but reduce expenses by shipping or bringing empty packaging to use in your booth display.

- If you bring or rent tables, save money by bringing your own table linens. Go to a local craft store and buy fabric that works with your brand colors. This also makes your booth look more cohesive. The colors of linens available for rent from the trade show facility may be limited. Make sure you get enough fabric to cover the top, sides, and fronts of your tables. Also, your booth will look much more professional if you spend ten minutes ironing out any wrinkles before setting out materials in your booth. If you pack the tablecloths in your luggage, bring a small iron in case your hotel doesn't provide one in the room.

✼ Check the trade show guide provided by trade show management after you sign up to determine whether any of your booth materials must be fireproofed in accordance with regulations. If so, search online for fireproofing companies in your area. Bring a copy of your fireproofing certificate with you in case the fire marshal spot-checks for compliance.

NEW-COMPANY BOOTH

Some trade shows offer a limited number of discounted spaces for new companies. This is a great bargain for smaller companies and a benefit to buyers actively seeking new and interesting companies. These booth spaces are often smaller than the typical one, which can actually reduce concern over how to fill them and make them look inviting on a limited budget. Not surprisingly, though, these spaces go quickly. If you're interested in exhibiting at a specific show, submit your application as soon as possible to try to grab one of these coveted spots.

NEW-PRODUCT DISPLAY AREA

Some shows offer a display area dedicated to showcasing products new to the market within the last year. This area is free of exhibitor booths and business owners trying to pitch their products so press and buyers tend to linger longer. If your trade show has such an area, you may showcase your product at an additional cost and under specified guidelines. This first glimpse may entice buyers to visit your booth to learn more. At some shows, attendees can even write down or scan information related to the companies that interest them. In these instances, even if you don't have a chance to meet with the buyer in person during the event, you'll receive their contact information after the show and can follow up then.

SAMPLING

Buyers may request to sample your product to make sure it tastes good! Read the trade show rules in full in advance so that you know what health permits you may need on hand to allow sampling. At a food-specific trade show, its representatives normally ensure the proper measures are already in place. Even so, plan to have plenty of tasting spoons, cups, napkins—whatever allows samples without anyone touching your product. Also consider bringing or renting a garbage can for your booth for used utensils. If you're attending a trade show that is not specific to the food industry, you may be required to set up a hand-washing station at your booth or provide antibacterial soap.

The key with samples of any kind is *not* to hand them out to everyone who passes by. At one trade show, I saw a company's twenty-foot corner booth (a substantial cost for them to rent) around which they strategically placed product samples. At first, one might think that getting product into as many hands as possible is a good thing, but these poor entrepreneurs ran out of samples by two in the afternoon on the first day of a three-day show. With no way to get more samples shipped to the site, how many potential buyers do you think they missed with two days left to go? How professional do you think their booth looked filled with big, empty display cartons?

Be prepared to qualify buyers before handing them samples. It can be as simple as giving samples only to buyers who come into your booth and actually engage with you. You might want to put additional parameters on this, such as how buyers respond to specific questions first. The choice is yours, but just make sure you pack enough samples.

PRACTICE YOUR PITCH

Practice your marketing pitch in advance of the show so that you'll be ready from day one. This is especially critical for small businesses that only attend one or two trade shows a year. Several months may have passed since your last show, and though you know your company's story and sales pitch, getting the words out concisely and in a compelling manner can be difficult. Try to develop a sales pitch that has you closing the sale by the end. For example, phrases like "Is there additional information I can send you after the show?" or "Are you interested in writing an order?" can help to convert someone who's browsing into someone who's buying. As they say, practice really does make perfect. After spending the time and money to participate in a trade show, you want to be sure that your sales pitch is perfect from the first day to the last.

HIRING SHOW STAFF

If at all possible, find another person to work the trade show with you. Even if you're the only person working on the business right now, you might have a good friend or a family member who would be willing to join you for all or part of the show. Having help gives you a chance to use the bathroom and walk around to see what other exhibitors have to offer. Be sure to share with your show partner your marketing message, your goals for the show, and whether you're offering any specials.

Hiring outside sales staff requires some comfort with employing some- one you don't know who doesn't know your product or company and allow- ing them to interact with buyers. This can be a very tricky situation unless you're confident that you can quickly get someone up to speed. Keep in mind, however, that rent-by-the-hour staff will never be as passionate about your company as you are. And you can never know exactly how professional new hires are until they arrive at the show.

DEVELOP YOUR TRADE SHOW MARKETING COLLATERAL

Getting the buyers to your booth is just the first step. Assuming that your booth and your sales pitch hook the buyer, you also want to send the buyer along with information about your company. Unless buyers have worked with you in the past, most will not place an order the first time they visit your booth. Buyers prefer to walk the show floor first, picking up materials about the companies that catch their attention. If you're lucky, the buyer will return to the hotel room and review material with the intent to place orders before leaving. Many buyers, however, will take the paperwork back to the hotel or office, sift through it for the most compelling companies, and then save the remaining information in a file for later. In any case, you want to make the cut. To improve your chances, make your trade show marketing material (which includes your company's marketing brochure and wholesale price list) as eye-catching and professional as your product.

LET YOUR CONTACTS KNOW YOU'RE COMING

It's smart to keep a database of wholesale contacts with whom you do business (or would like to). Reach out to let them know you'll be attending an upcoming trade show. You can use a direct mail piece, e-mail, or your e-newsletter. Be sure to include a hook that will entice them to come see you—such as a tip on any new product you might be offering—and don't forget to include your booth number.

Of course, just because you're going to the trade show doesn't mean all your contacts will attend. As you well know, it costs time and money for you to participate; the same holds true for buyers, and they simply can't go to all of them. So, if you plan to offer trade show attendees a specific promotion for orders placed at the event, consider offering the same promotion to your existing buyers. This is a great way of building trust: it shows your current buyers that you will always offer them the best possible pricing and promotions. It also encourages them to place an order now to take advantage of the promotion rather than wait. If you do this, make sure that your show promotion is clearly outlined in any preshow marketing materials sent to existing contacts so that they know the offer is available to them regardless of attendance.

> If there's a key industry trade show that you won't be attending but you know many of your contacts will, send out a direct mail piece, e-mail, or e-newsletter offering a "no-show special." In it, explain that although you won't be at the show, you're offering a special promotion during the show that they're welcome to take advantage of.

CREATE A TRADE SHOW PRESS KIT

Most trade shows have a press room where qualified media can stop in and pick up materials left by exhibiting companies. While you won't be allowed in the press room yourself, be sure that your company is represented there. The goal of the press kit is to capture the interest of journalists and bloggers, to provide them with basic information about your company, and to motivate them to come to your booth to meet you in person—or, at the very least, to follow up with you after the show.

- A summary sheet that concisely tells your company's story and provides the press with a hook: Why should they cover your company, and why now? Include here any awards or accolades you've received. Also include a short personal bio, since you as the entrepreneur are crucial to the business.

- A current press release written in traditional press release format that features the who, the what, the when, the where, the why, and the how of your company, along with another "hook"—something that will interest the press enough to follow up with you. Numerous websites are dedicated to the specifics of crafting a press release, so learn them there if you're not familiar.

- High-resolution product images with a note that press can contact you for the rights to use those pictures and/or other images you may have.

- Your contact information. It should go without saying that if you ever receive an e-mail from a press contact, you need to respond to it as soon as possible, because he or she may be working on a tight deadline. If you don't respond quickly enough, that person might move on to feature another company or product.

- A sample size of your product as appropriate, if you can afford it. Some entrepreneurs staple a sample-size package to the press kit itself to ensure that no one walks away with just the samples but no information.

- Your booth number. Journalists and bloggers often go to the press room prior to hitting the show floor. What they pick up there might help direct them your way. Inclusion of your booth number is especially critical at larger shows where there may be thousands of booths.

INVITE KEY MEDIA TO YOUR BOOTH

Before a show, reach out to journalists and bloggers who you feel might be key in spreading your message and invite them to visit your booth. Use e-mail or social media channels, especially if you've developed a relationship beforehand. As always, keep your target consumer in mind as you compile your list of influential press. Be prepared to explain why you think they should come to your booth and what benefit your product will bring to their audience.

Talking with Bloggers at Trade Shows

Bloggers play an increasingly important role in the promotion of products. Some bloggers may ask you, during trade shows, whether you'd be willing to donate product samples that they can use in giveaways on their site. If asked and you're unfamiliar with the blog, ask for their business card or information and let the blogger know that you will follow up shortly. This allows you the time to research the blog before making a determination as to whether or not it makes strategic sense to run a promotion with that blogger and, if so, what type of promotion offers you the best return-on-investment given your business and marketing goals.

SIGN UP FOR A BADGE-SCANNING DEVICE

Larger trade shows now offer exhibitors the opportunity to rent scanning devices that can compile buyer information based on the buyer's name tag. While this may initially sound intrusive, more and more buyers are leaving their business cards at home, counting on exhibitors to have these devices at events. The technology works as follows: a code is printed on each trade show attendee name tag that contains the contact information for that person. When scanned, that information is uploaded into a database for the exhibitor so that they have the information on file. Over the years, as buyers become more comfortable with the concept and the technology, sellers may look unprofessional if they don't use the device. Further, using a scanner keeps buyers from having to fumble around for business cards.

ADVERTISE IN THE SHOW GUIDE

Many trade shows produce a guide for attendees that includes the event floor plan, a schedule of events, and advertisements from exhibiting companies. They can provide an easy means to get your product and your company in front of buyers who may not be familiar with you otherwise.

Because these advertisements don't come cheap, though, consider your budget, the show demographics, and your own business goals.

- You must create (or hire someone to create) a professional advertisement. Any photography needs to be top-notch, your key selling feature must be clearly defined, and the ad itself should pop. The guide typically includes many advertisements, and you don't want your ad to get lost.

- If you offer a special show-related rate or promotion, if you are a new vendor, or if you have a new product, make sure that information is clearly called out in your ad.

- Include your booth number. Though this sounds like a simple detail, people often forget to include it or update it in a reused ad. Don't make buyers have to hunt for you.

- Include contact information such as your website and e-mail address. You can't meet all buyers at the event, but many take show guides home, so give them a way to get in touch with you afterward.

- To cut costs, consider taking out a group ad. For example, you and seven other entrepreneurs could go in together and create a color, full-page ad at one-eighth of the cost each. Think about ways to tie together in a group ad. If your products are all made in the United States, for instance, a related tag line might make sense.

Show guides aren't the only publications given out at trade shows. At larger shows, various trade and business magazines pass out free copies. Some even publish special, show-specific editions. Some of these magazines sell ad space, which means that their subscribers could see your ad along with show attendees. This approach might be an especially effective use of marketing dollars if it suits your budget.

Last, advertising deadlines for show guides and trade publications are usually several months in advance. When you decide to attend a show, look into advertising deadlines and mark them on your calendar so that your ad will be ready when needed.

EVENT SPONSORSHIP

At many trade shows, participants may sponsor a portion of the event for a fee. Typically, several levels of sponsorship are available. For example, a cheese company might sponsor the happy-hour wine event for buyers after the show closes each day. Sponsorships are usually expensive, so make sure that you understand what they entail. What sort of recognition will your company get? Will your logo be included on the trade show's website, print material, or elsewhere? Can you include a promotional piece in the trade show goody bags given to press and/or attendees? Know what your sponsorship gets you and decide if the return on investment is worthwhile. If it interests you, contact show management well in advance to learn more and to secure your spot as early as possible to take full advantage of the benefits.

PRE-PROMOTE ONLINE

Since you can never be 100 percent sure about how a buyer might learn about your company, include your booth number on your website and on social media channels. Even if your online persona is more consumer-focused, you never know who might look at your site or check out your company's Facebook page. Buyers are sometimes given advance access to the list of exhibitors from which they can research a company's online presence to determine which booths they plan to visit at the show.

MIMES, FLYING MONKEYS, AND FOOTBALL GAMES

If you attend enough trade shows, you'll begin to notice exhibitors who pull out every trick in the book in an attempt to get people to notice their booths. Some rent celebrities or actors (both human and animal). Others install televisions in their booths and show the latest football game or other sporting event. It's easy to get caught up in such over-the-top attempts to get noticed.

Don't go down that route unless there's a direct tie-in to your product. If a celebrity has endorsed your product and you can afford to hire him or her to attend, then it may make sense to bring that person to the show. Hiring a celebrity just for the sake of it, however, does little for your brand or your company. You may attract attendees eager to have their photos taken, but do you think those people will remember your company—or their celebrity encounter?

Doing something that attracts a huge crowd can backfire on you. At one food industry trade show, an exhibitor installed a television to show the football play-offs. This may have made sense if their brand appealed primarily to a male audience. But the truth of the matter is, I couldn't tell you a thing about their brand because I was never able to get near it. So many people were standing around watching the game that they actually spilled out of the booth and blocked access to the corridor. Few, if any, in the crowd were focused on the company or the product. With so many people in the way, interested buyers couldn't get close enough to talk with salespeople and learn more.

PULL TOGETHER A TRADE SHOW EMERGENCY KIT

No matter how well you plan for a trade show, there's always a chance that something will go wrong. Put together an emergency kit so you're prepared for the most common trade show disasters.

DURING THE TRADE SHOW

The event has finally arrived. It's opening day, and you've worked so hard to prepare. The show floor is buzzing with energy and excitement. Everyone rushes to make last-minute touch-ups to their booths. It's game time.

Common Trade Show Emergency Kit Items

- Duct tape (it really will fix just about anything)
- Adhesive tape
- Stapler and staples
- Scissors
- Extra pens and/or pencils
- Calculator
- Needle and thread

WATCH YOUR BODY LANGUAGE

Though this may seem like stating the obvious, your body language and the body language of anyone helping at your booth can make or break your trade show experience. Attend a trade show on the last day when the exhibitors are all tired and worn down. Count how many people you see slumped in their chairs, standing around with their feet firmly planted and their arms crossed, or—and this happens more than you can imagine—reading a book, answering e-mails, or look-

> ✂ Safety pins
> ✂ Aspirin and/or allergy medicine
> ✂ Water bottle
> ✂ Nonperishable snacks
> ✂ Gum and/or breath mints
> ✂ Small iron (if one isn't provided in your hotel room)

ing otherwise distracted by their smartphones or other electronic devices. If you're a buyer with a multitude of products from which to choose, how likely are you to step into the booth of a slumped individual to strike up a conversation? Smile! It can make all the difference.

KEEP SALES MATERIALS CLOSE

Don't hand out those beautiful marketing brochures you worked so hard to create to just anyone passing by. Remember that those brochures cost you money. Give them to those who appear genuinely interested in your company. Many trade show veterans keep their marketing brochures inside their booths rather than on the outer edges. This forces prospective buyers to step into the booth for brochures. This not only reveals true interest, it also presents you with an opportunity to initiate a conversation.

LISTEN MORE THAN YOU TALK

Once someone expresses an interest in your product, it can be tempting to let loose the pitch you spent hours practicing, giving all the details about your company. But you could miss out on an opportunity to explain why your product is a perfect fit for a buyer's particular store. How can you know what the store needs if you don't find out about it first?

Remember that every buyer is different and has different needs. Your job is to find out what those needs are and then to tweak your pitch in a way that shows how your product or company can fill that need. Ask the buyer about who the store's customers are, how it's set up, and how it merchandises its product offerings. If you can, find out if the store conducts category reviews before bringing on a new product or if it's open to adding new products right away. Learn about what price points customers are comfortable paying and what margins the store looks for.

For example, when Buyer A comes steps into your booth, it may not be evident from a name badge alone that his or her store has been getting more and more requests for environmentally friendly gift items. Once you uncover this information, you can craft your pitch around the environmentally sound packaging that you use and the steps you're taking to reduce waste in your company. Buyer B, on the other hand, runs a store focused on selling quality products at an affordable price. In that case, you might focus your pitch on your lower-priced products that would resonate better with Buyer B's customers. Asking questions and genuinely listening to the answers enables you to better assist the buyer. You have just a few minutes to capture a buyer's attention on a busy trade show floor. You must uncover the problem each particular buyer is trying to solve and then provide the solution.

MAKE CONNECTIONS WHEN POSSIBLE

While you're listening to the buyer, look and listen for clues that might help you to build connections. Check out the buyer's name badge. If the store location is included on the badge and you recognize it—maybe you used to live there, you have friends there, you've visited, or you would like to visit—mention your connection. Similarly, sometimes a buyer will let it slip that his or her current role is a change of career. This presents the perfect opportunity for you to share your own story. Do what you can to make connections. This gets conversation flowing. Keep in mind, though, that these connections must be genuine. Otherwise, you'll come off sounding like a used-car salesperson.

PREPARE TO PERSONALIZE YOUR FOLLOW-UP

You've done everything possible to answer the buyer's questions, to address his or her needs, and to make a connection. Still, the buyer isn't quite ready to place an order. Don't worry. You were able to get the buyer to notice you, and that's the first step. The second step is up to you. To follow up after the trade show, get contact information either using the badge-scanner or by asking for a business card. After the buyer walks away with your marketing material and price sheet, take a moment to write down specifics from your conversation. Write directly on the business card or on the printout produced by the badge-scanning device. The note could be as trivial as a shared dislike of tomatoes, the buyer's upcoming trip to Kenya, or—if you're lucky—the specific problem that the buyer is looking to solve. These notes will help you to personalize follow-up conversations you have after the trade show.

> **Tip!**
>
> While you're at the trade show, have someone take a photo of you and any booth staff in your booth with big smiles all around. Include this picture with your initial follow-up e-mail. After a long trade show, this is a great way to remind buyers of who you are. They probably just met and spoke with many, many exhibitors. Names and faces can easily blur together. A personal note plus a photo will help you to stand out.

BE ON THE LOOKOUT FOR TROLLERS

A few trollers exist at every show. They walk the show floor picking up every sales brochure, price list, and sample they can get their hands on with no real intention of placing an order. It's easy to lose a number of samples or a stack of marketing materials to these folks, which is another reason to try to determine if a buyer is seriously interested before handing anything over. Trollers also like to get into long-winded stories about their eighteen cats, for instance. Though they may be well meaning and harmless, trollers can be in the midst of a trivial tale when the one buyer you've been hoping to meet stops by your booth. Prepare a way to gently exit the conversation with the storyteller so that you can transfer your attention to the buyer. This can be as simple as saying, "Would you excuse me for one minute? I'm working this booth by myself. Do you mind if I help these people and come back to you?"

It goes without saying that you should always be polite, regardless of whom you're talking to. The distinction between a troller and a genuine buyer is not always obvious. One notorious story is that of a prestigious buyer and his wife who attended a trade show. His name was recognizable to most everyone there; the wife, on the other hand, had a different last name and was therefore unknown to most exhibitors. As they walked the trade show floor, the buyer would get pulled into conversations with eager exhibitors, but the wife was more or less disregarded and left alone. She wandered the trade show corridors looking at booths and talking to people, but when asked, she would clearly state that she had no decision-making power with regard to purchasing for her husband's store. Though the woman may not have been the one making final decisions, she certainly had the ear of the buyer. As trade show lore has it, she ended up bringing her husband around the next day to talk only with the exhibitors who had treated her respectfully the day before. Whether this actually happened or whether it's simply a trade show myth, one can't be sure. Regardless, it presents a good lesson to remember that you never know whom you're dealing with, so you should always treat everyone with respect.

WALK THE SHOW FLOOR

Walking the show floor can help get you out of your booth and clear your head. It also gives you a chance to take a look around, see what your competitors are doing, and see where the industry as a whole is headed. It might even spark ideas for your next trade show exhibit.

As you walk around, look for early signs of trends that might be emerging, as this might give you ideas about new products to design or develop. Just as fashion experts attend fashion shows to determine the season's hemline height and color scheme, you can look for similar information. For example, if you notice spicy-sweet flavor combinations everywhere, now might be the time to add a spicy-sweet product to your line. Keep your eyes open for a variety of clues and ideas about what buyers and consumers are looking for now. This information might enable you to spot or even get ahead of the next top-selling trend.

Your walk also presents a great opportunity to look at how other booths are designed. File that information away for your next trade show. You might find a great piece of functional furniture that you'd like to incorporate. You might find that the flow of another company's small booth space is a great fit for your booth and product concept. Looking to others for design ideas and inspiration will only help make your booth that much better the next time you exhibit.

Beside the design of their booths, take a moment to look at what your competitors are doing in them. What new products are they introducing? What packaging are they using? For obvious reasons, don't pretend to be a buyer and pump your competitor for information. Don't try to grab their marketing brochure or price list. Simply by looking at their booth and product offerings you can gather insights and see opportunities that you can use for your business.

Last, the trade show floor gives you the chance to meet other small exhibitors. If they don't appear busy when you walk by, take a moment to introduce yourself and ask how the show is going. This is your chance to develop relationships with other entrepreneurs who you might not meet otherwise. Small food business owners, I've found, are usually more than willing to share ideas and information with other entrepreneurs. These people may become some of the best allies you have in the industry.

EAT WELL AND GET YOUR REST

It's amazing how tiring standing on your feet all day with a smile on your face can be. If you have help during the show, make sure you take breaks during the day to sit down away from the eyes of buyers. If you don't have anyone with you, make sure that you arrive each day with enough food and water to get you through. At night, go to bed early and get your rest. You've got another long day ahead of you.

DON'T FORGET THAT YOU'RE ALWAYS ON

At the trade show, you'll likely be wearing a name tag that includes your company's name. You might also wear some of your company's paraphernalia, like a T-shirt or a baseball hat with your company logo. So when you step away from your booth to take a phone call and end up yelling at the plumber on the other end who called to say that your house just flooded, buyers walking by are listening. Even if your rants and screams seem entirely legitimate, is that the impression that you want buyers to have of you and your company?

Similarly, when you step into the bathroom at a trade show, there are more than likely potential buyers in the room. Be sure to wash your hands well (not that you don't already), and don't leave a flooded sink or throw trash on the floor. And when the show's over for the day and you're headed back to your hotel, watch what you say. In the flood of people headed out of the doors, you're likely surrounded by at least a few buyers. If you're staying in a hotel near the trade show, make sure you maintain your very best manners every time you leave your room. You never know who will be riding in the elevator with you.

AFTER THE TRADE SHOW

The trade show is over, and you did everything possible before and during the show to make it a success. Unfortunately, despite the fact that you're probably exhausted, you've still got more work to do. In addition to filling any orders you received at the show, you need to follow up with your leads and press contacts within a week of the show's end. Otherwise, all of your hard work and money could go to waste.

BUSINESS LEADS

If the show went well, you probably have contact information for some retail buyers, distributors, and brokers or sales reps who are interested in learning more about your company. If you kept careful notes during the show about the specific interests of each party, now is the time to send a personalized e-mail with the information each requested.

You may also have met buyers who shared their contact information with you but didn't ask for any specific follow-up information. To those individuals, send a quick e-mail reminding them of what you and your company have to offer, your main selling features, and offer to send any additional information they may need. Ideally, do some research on each contact and try to make a connection with them in your e-mails. For example, if you're reaching out to a Midwestern company, mention your own Midwest roots in the e-mail. Again, the key here is to be and sound genuine rather than "salesy." Your goal is to start building relationships.

BUSINESS CONTACTS YOU DIDN'T MEET

If you went into the show hoping to meet key buyers who would be good fits for your product but missed someone, take advantage of the attendee contact information list that many shows offer following the show. Send a "sorry I missed you" e-mail (or traditional mail if no e-mail address is included) providing a quick piece about your company and your products. Also ask about requirements for submitting a product for review.

PRESS

Once again, hopefully you took good notes during the show so that you can immediately follow up with any press contacts who came by your booth. For press in particular, it's best to follow up no more than two days after the show closes. If someone made a specific request, you certainly want to get them the material—samples, press-ready photographs, and so forth—as soon as possible. Though the press member may not be working on deadline, you don't want to miss being included in a piece just because you took too long to respond.

If a press contact didn't request any specific information, do your homework on what publication he or she writes or produces for and send a follow-up e-mail with a soft hook, including the reason he or she should want to write about you, with an emphasis on their audience. Again, include a picture of you in your trade show booth to help jog his or her memory. Even if these contacts aren't ready to write about you at the moment, begin to follow what they do write about. Engage with them via social media (if they're open to that) and try to build a relationship so that when the timing's right, you'll be the one they call.

FINAL NOTES ON TRADE SHOWS

No matter how well you prepare or how much follow-up you do, not every show will be a winner. This can be very disheartening to small business owners, especially since they've poured their hearts and souls into their products and their companies. Further, participation in a trade show may have eaten a large hole in their limited marketing budgets. Don't let a bad show get you down for too long, though.

Keep the following things in mind: Maybe the show you attended didn't reach your target audience. No matter what you'd hoped, your barbeque sauce company just didn't play well at the vegan trade show. Now you know, and you won't return to the show again. You can say you tried it and move on.

It's also possible that you interacted with the right audience, but people simply didn't place orders. In this case, take what you learned from buyers about what they liked and didn't like about your product and/or packaging. Now you can make changes as needed. If you do decide to make changes, be sure to follow up with your show contacts to let them know about the modifications and to see if your revised product is now a better fit for them.

TRADE SHOW CHECKLIST

Six to twelve months in advance:

- Visit shows in advance if possible, taking note of the buyers attending and the booth displays

- Put down deposits to participate in the shows that meet your demographic needs

- Get organized and prepare to receive lots of paperwork

- Determine specific goals for each show

- Begin preliminary booth design

- Develop a preshow marketing plan

- Book freight arrangements if necessary

- Book hotel, flight, and other travel arrangements as needed

- Have professional photos taken if needed

Three to four months in advance:

- Finalize booth display

- Develop and print marketing collateral including sales kit, price list, and booth signage

- Create and print out press kit

🖊 Submit preshow advertising in accordance with ad deadlines

🖊 Design preshow marketing materials such as direct mail or direct e-mail pieces

🖊 Pay final booth fee (verify their exact deadlines), rent carpeting, electricity, booth furniture, or other items as necessary

🖊 Double-check show guidelines and make sure you understand all move-in and move-out instructions

🖊 Add trade show information and booth number to your website, your e-mail signature, social media, and other channels as appropriate

Three to four weeks in advance:

🖊 Finalize press release

🖊 Communicate sales pitch and messaging to booth staff

🖊 Send out preshow marketing materials to existing contacts and key press

🖊 Develop your post show follow-up plan and accompanying material, such as an e-mail template

🖊 Ship freight to trade show if applicable (coordinate with freight company's schedule)

Two weeks in advance:

🖊 Ensure there's a plan in place to keep your company running smoothly while you're away

⚡ Create an out-of-office e-mail reply that includes your booth number

⚡ Check and double-check your trade show emergency kit

⚡ Ship any additional trade show materials (such as booth materials) to hotel or exhibit site if mailing directly

One to two days in advance:

⚡ Set up booth

⚡ Deliver press kit to press office

⚡ Meet and network with other vendors

⚡ Place your product in the new product showcase if applicable

⚡ Attend vendor seminars and educational sessions of interest to you as time allows

⚡ Practice your pitch over and over until it feels natural to you and your staff

During the trade show:

⚡ Smile

⚡ Engage with buyers, distributors, brokers, and press—ask questions, build relationships, and share what makes your product and your company great

⚡ Listen to learn about buyers' needs and to get feedback about your product

- Take notes concerning contacts you'll want to follow up with after the show

- Drink lots of fluids, eat healthfully, and gets lots of rest

After the show:

- Follow up with press as soon as possible

- Follow up with contacts and institute post show marketing plan

- Evaluate whether or not the show met your expectations and helped you meet your goals

- Decide whether or not you want to attend the show again

CONCLUSION

SELLING WHOLESALE CAN BE EXTREMELY lucrative for your food business, but as shown in this book, it also takes a lot of work to accomplish in a smart, strategic manner. If I can share one last piece of advice—while your vision may be to see your product on store shelves across the country, more often than not, I see amazing and delicious food brands expand too quickly before they have the capital to support such growth. Take the time to grow your local and regional sales so that you can rely on that revenue or on interest from potential angel investors to help your brand grow to national sales. The time will also allow you to fine-tune your sales and marketing message, develop relationships with brokers and distributors, and find a copacker who can keep production on pace with your growth or grow your staff so you can handle higher production in-house.

I invite you to visit the Small Food Business website (www.smallfoodbiz. com) for more information about running and growing a food business and I look forward to buying your products on a store shelf in the near future!

55467164R00093

Made in the USA
San Bernardino,
CA